JAMS

WITH A TWIST

JAMS
WITH A TWIST

Deliciously different
recipes for sweet surprises

KYLEE NEWTON

 National Trust

Published by National Trust Books
An imprint of HarperCollins Publishers
1 London Bridge Street, London SE1 9GF
www.harpercollins.co.uk

HarperCollins Publishers
1st Floor, Watermarque Building, Ringsend Road, Dublin 4, Ireland

First published 2022

ISBN 978-1-91-165738-5
10 9 8 7 6 5 4 3 2 1

A catalogue record for this book is available from the British Library.
Printed in India

MIX
Paper from
responsible sources
FSC™ C007454

This book is produced from independently certified
FSC™ paper to ensure responsible forest management.

For more information visit: www.harpercollins.co.uk/green

If you would like to comment on any aspect of this book, please contact us at
the above address or national.trust@harpercollins.co.uk

National Trust publications are available at National Trust shops or online at
nationaltrustbooks.co.uk

Contents

Introduction

When asked to write a jams book for the National Trust, how could I resist? The National Trust has always protected nature, beauty and history so that they can be enjoyed by everyone. I believe preserving and jam making go hand in hand with this approach. Jam preserves nature at its peak to feed us when a season has passed its best.

These aren't your typical jams. The Trust wanted a guide to making jams with a twist, and I assured them that they had come to the right person. For more than eight years, I have been passionate about turning fruits and vegetables into delicious treats, using a contemporary approach and adapting the old-fashioned recipes of yesteryear to suit a more modern palate. I was lucky enough to explore the many delights of experimenting with flavour combinations in *The Modern Preserver*, but in this book I've had the chance to create something even more fun and offer further twists and turns to get you excited about the preserving process.

In the following pages, I'll take you through five deliciously different takes on your preserving practice: Flavour Twists; Pick to Preserve; Jelly Floats; The Layered Effect and Sundae Fun-day. Whether you are new to jam making or an old hand, you will learn to: balance flavour combinations; go foraging in your garden and further afield for ingredients; create two-tone and traffic light layers in your jars; and float fruit, flowers and herbs in your jellies. Lastly, and the biggest twist, there's a whole chapter of all your favourite classic jammy desserts packed into jars!

THE CHEMISTRY OF JAM

By the 1800s, when sugar became more readily available, it was relatively easy to make homemade jams – usually by matching fruit weight to sugar weight. But times have changed, and this measurement ratio is becoming a thing of the past. Today we are more health conscious and aim to reduce the sugar content in our diets. Jam makers have therefore started to look more closely at the science and rely more on the natural chemical reaction that happens to the pectin in fruit (see page 9) when mixed with citric acid and heat. Sugar is still necessary, as it draws water away from the pectin, which aids gelling. Less water also means a lower chance of a microbial growth environment, which in turn helps with the longevity of jams and jellies. So, although you'll see a reduction in sugar in modern recipes, it's still necessary for achieving natural preservation and to be legally allowed to call your product a 'jam'.

I tend to work on the ratio of 40% added sugar weight to 60% fruit weight. Depending on the fruit used and its natural sugar content (fructose), this tends to give you a 60–70% final sugar content, which binds enough of the water to call it a jam. Jams that contain less than 60–65% 'final sugars' are called conserves, compotes or fruit spreads. These preserves, with their lower sugar content, will only keep if a good practice of heat seal sterilisation is followed (see below) and they will degrade quicker, in or out of the fridge, once opened.

Often, I find, older generations in my classes and demos challenge the idea of the sterilisation process – 'In our day we never sterilised our jars; the jams never went off and lasted for years.' The modern way is to use 'hot fill' sterilisation, because with less added sugar than more traditional jams we rely on a different type of chemistry to give jams longevity. This cleaner practice tends to kill off any unwanted bacteria that might spoil the jam (see below for more details).

Bacteria and sterilisation

Bacteria exist in and on everything, from the air to our food. The good thing is that bacteria die at temperatures of 65°C/149°F and hotter, and become dormant and unable to reproduce at -18°C/-0.4°F. From 0–5°C/32–41°F, bacteria are 'sleepy' and reproduce at a much slower rate, hence the reason food still degrades at lower temperatures, such as in the fridge – just more slowly. At temperatures of 5–63°C/41–145°F, bacteria are at their most active; this is when fermentation comes into play, when we want the 'good' bacteria to work for us to help break down produce.

The practice of 'hot fill' sterilisation is when you wash your jars and lids in hot soapy water, rinse them, drip-dry them upside down, and then place them (right side up) in a preheated low oven at 100°C/90°C fan/gas ¼ for at least 20 minutes (anything higher can burn the rubber seal of the lids, or not match the temperature of your jam, and breakages can happen). This process works on the principle that when you fill the jars, straight from the oven, with hot jam of around the same temperature (100–104°C/212–219°F) and seal them immediately, you create an environment where bacteria can't survive, or potentially grow before sealing. As soon as you open that seal, the jam becomes exposed to bacteria in the air, and so from then on the jar needs to be stored in the fridge.

Pectin and citric acid

Pectin is a natural binding substance, found in fruits and some vegetables, which joins cells together to create their skins. It also comes in handy when making jam, as it's responsible for the set of your jam by 'gelling up' the cooked pulped fruit once it's cooled. Citric acid, such as lemon juice, is commonly added to the jamming process as it helps to create a good pH level of 2.8–3.3; this, plus heat, helps the pectin to react and start gelling.

The tricky thing is that all fruits contain different levels of pectin and acid, so it takes knowledge, practice and a bit of a balancing act to get the right formula. You can find a lot of good fruit pectin/ acid charts online to guide you. All is not lost if your set isn't firm; looser, soft-set jams have many good uses, and are sometimes nicer than over-processed commercial jams that are set almost like gelatinous jellies.

THE JAM/JELLY PROCESS

Equipment

It does pay to invest in a large jam/preserving/maslin pan, although it is not entirely essential. These pans are designed with a larger circumference on the top rim and a smaller circumference on the heavy base, which allows for quicker evaporation and therefore better results. I work with large 9-litre/15¾-pint stainless-steel jam pans, although traditionally people used copper pans. Copper pans are great conductors of heat, so are a good way to control the jam temperature – however, unless the pan is lined with stainless steel, I tend to taste the metal of the copper in my jam, so I avoid them. If you don't have a jam pan, choose a large-rimmed, heavy-based pot or pan, with low sides, large enough for the quantity of fruit and sugar, plus double, to allow room for the jam to boil up.

Other handy bits and bobs are: long-handled wooden spoons (the longer the better, as jam spits and burns); small saucers (for the set test – see page 14); large muslin squares (cheesecloth and/or a jelly drip bag for making jelly); culinary string; kitchen scales; chopping board; sharp cook's knife; paring knife; lemon squeezer and tea strainer. Jelly can be tricky to set; I use a sugar thermometer to help me, as it allows me to measure exactly when the jelly temperature reaches 104°C/219°F.

Also, when it comes to jarring, essential tools are a metal jam-jar funnel and a metal ladle (I always sterilise these along with my jars as an extra precaution). However, a Perspex jug or heatproof plastic or metal jug will suffice. Lastly, I couldn't make jam without my Ove Gloves. Everything you handle when making jam is hot and needs handling with care; tea towels or oven gloves will do, but the Ove Gloves have fingers that give you more control.

Jars and lids

You can buy new jars and lids online or at good cookery shops. However, if you have a collection of pre-used or vintage jars and lids, then these are useful – especially if you want to be kinder to the planet. So, re-use old jars and lids but make sure that they don't have any cracks or chips and have been thoroughly cleaned, rinsed and sterilised (see page 9). Inspect the rubber seals of your pre-used lids. Make sure they don't look discoloured or dry, aren't smelly and don't have any cracks that might compromise a secure seal. If in doubt, new lids often come in generic sizes to fit all jars, so just buy them – button/pop lids are best for hot preserves as these suction down and indicate a secure seal. I also cut non-stick baking paper caps to cover the surface of jams before sealing.

Fruit

Fruit loses its pectin as it ripens, so choose fresh and just ripe or slightly underripe fruit to help you with your setting needs. Jamming frozen berries and rhubarb works well, so if you find yourself with freshly picked berries, freeze them – as close to picking as you can. Defrost, then omit any water stated in the recipe as frozen fruit will retain a lot of liquid.

Don't cook more than 3kg/6lb 8oz of fruit at a time. Although it's tempting when you have a large glut of one thing, you will struggle to achieve a set because the temperature will never get to the heat required for the pectin to react efficiently – unless you have commercial equipment which controls the temperature throughout.

Get to know the pectin and acid levels of different fruits. Some fruits that are higher in pectin are great to mix with others that are lower in pectin to achieve a successful set.

Sugar

When it comes to jamming, I'm a bit of a purist, meaning that I like to use white granulated or caster sugar. I want the fruit to be the hero, so I don't like to compromise its flavour by experimenting with coconut, raw or brown sugars. By all means, though, play around with the different complexities that different sugars can create in your jams.

Jam and preserving sugar are available from most supermarkets and online. Jam sugar contains added pectin and citrus acid to aid any low-pectin or overripe fruits, so use it with strawberries or rhubarb to create firmer sets. Preserving sugar has larger granules, which are perfect when using citrus fruits and making jelly, and it dissolves more slowly, lessening the need to stir and therefore creating a clearer, brighter preserve for floating ingredients to be observed.

Prep

Always wash your fruit. I then like to cut everything into bite-sized pieces, not much bigger than 1–3cm/½–1¼in cubes. This allows the fruit to break down into a pulpy state and reach the required temperature more quickly, so the fructose (sugar) levels of the fruit don't release too much with overcooking and the nutrition and colour of the fruit aren't jeopardised.

Remove skins and stones/pips where needed and keep your berries whole (unless they are super-sized, in which case halve or quarter them). If you like chunky bits in your jam, reserve some of the fruit chunks or berries until just after the stage of dissolving in the sugar.

Cooking

There are plenty of different jamming techniques out there, each offering varying degrees of success. Find the one that works best for you and which gives you the best results. Some recipes ask you to macerate softer fruits with the sugar first for 8–12 hours; I like to do this when infusing fruit with delicate herbs or flowers, so that their flavour penetrates the fruit. This also draws out the water for a reduced cooking time. Other recipes will advise adding water to help soften firmer fruits into a pulp first, or heating the sugar in the oven before adding so that it dissolves more quickly. Heat is key with jam, and all recipes require you to reach around 104°C/219°F – a vigorous, rolling boil that you can't stir down. This is necessary for water evaporation so that the pectin can congeal.

For best results, I get to a high temperature and my setting point as quickly as I can so that I'm not overcooking my jams, jellies or marmalades and I don't risk losing a lot of nutrition or flavour from the fruit. To do this, I soften my prepared fruit over a high heat, mostly with a little water, and make a pulp first, watching and stirring often at this stage so that it doesn't catch on the bottom and burn. I bring this pulp to the boil and stir through the sugar, stirring until completely dissolved. I then bring it back to a vigorous rolling boil over the highest heat possible, only stirring intermittently now as I don't want to cool the jam with each stir. I also don't want it to stick to the bottom of the pan and burn (which it will want to do). I really work my wooden spoon on the bottom of the pan to lift off any sticking that I can feel.

Set testing, jarring and storing

A lot of recipes will tell you to boil for a certain amount of time at 104°C/219°F. These timings are always an estimate because the writer will never know the actual pectin and acid content of your fruit, or the heat source and the pan that you are using. I find the best way to gauge when to start testing your jam for a set is to watch for the change in the boiling bubble. At the start of the boil it will be rapid with lots of little bubbles, but, as the pectin starts to congeal and thicken, the bubbles will become heavier as they start to struggle to get through to the surface – this is when you take the jam off the heat and do your set test.

To set (or wrinkle) test, place several small saucers in the freezer at least 1 hour before you start cooking. When ready to test, take a saucer from the freezer, place about ⅛ teaspoon of jam on the saucer and put it into the fridge for 1 minute. This mimics the cooling process. Remove from the fridge and gently push with your finger; if you see a wrinkle on the surface of the jam, then your jam is hard-set and ready to jar.

Some fruits (which are lower in pectin) don't often give a clear wrinkle and they will always make a soft-set jam. For these, use your forefinger to lift the jam off the saucer and look at how slowly it drips to judge the final consistency you desire. If the jam isn't ready to jar, return the pan to the highest heat and continue to boil and test every 1–3 minutes until it's at your desired set (soft or hard).

When ready to jar, quickly and carefully skim off any surface foam or scum with a spatula and discard. Stir through any flavour twists that you haven't already added, like alcohol or herbs and dried flowers that you wouldn't want to lose while skimming, then ladle into your hot jars using a funnel (or jug). Fill the jars with jam quite close to the rim (only 1–2mm from the very top), being as clean as possible. Clean the rim with a hot, damp cloth and seal with a sterilised lid immediately. Fill all the jars, scraping in all the end bits with a spatula. If you end up with a half-filled jar, seal as normal but place in the fridge when cooled and eat first.

Once cooled, label and date your jars and store in a cool, dark place. Jams, jellies and marmalades will keep for up to a year if correctly sterilised and sealed, but once opened store them in the fridge and eat within 1–2 months (if not sooner – you be the judge). Lower-sugar conserves and compotes will not last as long, so refer to the recipe's instructions on storage.

Chapter 1

Flavour Twists

A contemporary trend that's been taking over the jam community recently is the addition of a complementary flavour twist to a single-variety fruit base. This involves adding alcohol, herbs, flowers, essences, cordials, syrups, teas, spices, nuts, nibs, kernels or mixing different fruits together to bring a different element and flavour profile to your palate. It makes your jam practice creative and fun.

Much like baking, there's a range of flavours to explore when making jams, jellies and marmalades. With fruit, as with baking, I find it's best to stick to the classic flavour combinations: fundamentally, there's a reason they have become classics. So, if you're starting out on this journey of twists and turns, start there as a base. The more you learn, the more you'll find your palate open to new discoveries, where you can play with different medleys and infusions and become more adventurous.

⬩ If adding boozy infusions, stir through the measure at the end of cooking, just after skimming and before jarring. The alcohol burns off in the heat of the jam, leaving the flavour behind and making it child-friendly. Try limes with tequila, peaches with whisky and blackberries with Frangelico.

♦ Teas, syrups, cordials, essences and extracts also make great flavour twists. Experiment with them all to your desired taste. I like to brew a strong tea and add it instead of water at the beginning. When adding more concentrated flavours, I tend to add these at the end, after skimming and before jarring.

♦ Macerate chopped soft herbs or leaves, such as mint or basil, with prepped soft fruit, such as apricots and peaches, mixed with the measure of sugar, for 8–12 hours prior to cooking to allow the flavours to penetrate the fruit. This also works with fresh petalled flowers and some dried varieties that are meeker in strength, such as rose or elderflower. For sturdier herbs like rosemary or lemon thyme, add these plucked or finely chopped just before jarring, or tie up into a bouquet garni, pop them in while cooking and fish them out at the end.

♦ Be mindful with stronger floral additions such as lavender or violet. These flavours can sometimes overpower the fruit, so balance them with care so that one flavour does not dominate over another. Add them at the end, after skimming and before jarring, and they will infuse within the jar once sealed.

♦ Add spices just as you would in baking: cinnamon (ground or whole quills), cardamom seeds (gently crushed), ginger (ground or freshly grated), star anise, vanilla pod seeds, nutmeg and saffron. You can even try chilli flakes or freshly ground black pepper if you like a bit of zing in your breakfast jam. These are added at the start, to allow the spice to slowly release its essence while cooking; scoop them out just before jarring.

♦ Combine seasonal fruits together, matching sweet with tart or high pectin with low pectin. Try gooseberries with strawberries, rhubarb with raspberries, peaches with cranberries or mix up several fruits you have accumulating in your fruit bowl and make rainbow jam for a more festive preserve.

♦ Nuts, kernels, nibs and beans are also a fun addition, adding a new texture to your jam. Add flaked almonds or roughly chopped hazelnuts or cobnuts 10–15 minutes before the end of cooking so they don't lose too much crunch. Or add kernels from inside the stones of fruit, cocoa nibs or even roughly ground coffee beans for an interesting twist.

After following my few simple suggestions, and once you've got into the practice of adding additional flavours to your favourite fruits, you'll find yourself creating further weird and wonderful combinations. You'll soon be making an array of jams and jellies that suit your own tastes.

Baked Apricot and Toasted Almond Jam

MAKES 5–6 X 230ML/8FL OZ JARS | SUMMER | LOW PECTIN

Apricots, like strawberries, epitomise the idea of summer for me. As an avid preserver, this is the time to get busy; it's time to 'save the season' in jars of summery delights. Only when I have put the seasonal glut to good use can I kick off my shoes and go running barefoot on the beach.

1.2kg/2lb 11oz (pitted weight) apricots, *halved*

1 unwaxed lemon

50ml/2fl oz lemon juice, *freshly squeezed*

600g/1lb 5oz jam sugar

3 tbsp almond flakes, *toasted and patted dry*

Preheat the oven to 180°C/170°C fan/gas 4 and place several small saucers in the freezer.

Place the apricot halves on a baking sheet. Zest over the lemon and bake for 35–40 minutes to soften.

Turn the oven down to 100°C/90°C fan/gas ¼ to sterilise your jars and lids (see page 9).

Place the baked apricots and any baking juice in a jam pan with the lemon juice. Use a wooden spoon to break them up and bring to the boil over a medium-high heat. Stir so that they do not to stick and burn, and use your spoon to break the apricots into a pulp-like state.

When pulpy and spitting, pour in the jam sugar, stirring until the sugar dissolves completely. Bring back to the boil over the highest heat, stirring intermittently, feeling the bottom of the pan with your spoon so that the jam does not catch and burn.

Add the toasted almonds and cook on a rapid boil for 5–8 minutes. Remove from the heat and start set testing (see page 14) for a loose soft-set jam, where the jam slowly drops from your finger.

Once at the desired set, skim off any scum and ladle the hot jam into hot sterilised jars and seal (see page 15). Store unopened in a cool, dark place for up to a year. Once opened, keep in the fridge and eat within 1–2 months.

Peach and Basil Jam

MAKES 5–6 X 230ML/8FL OZ JARS | SUMMER | LOW PECTIN

Peach jam is often overly sweet, so to counteract this I like to add soft herbs to balance the sweetness. Try this recipe with any fresh herb that you might have to hand or in the garden, such as mint, marjoram or lemon verbena. Macerating the herbs with the fruit and sugar to begin with means that the herb's flavour can permeate into the fruit.

1.4kg/3lb 3oz peaches, *pitted weight*

12–14 large basil leaves, *finely chopped*

50ml/2fl oz lemon juice, *freshly squeezed*

700g/1lb 9oz jam sugar

1 unwaxed lemon, *grated zest*

Cut the peaches into 1–2cm/½–¾in cubes. Place in a bowl with the basil, lemon juice and sugar, cover and macerate overnight in the fridge.

The next day, sterilise your jars and lids (see page 9) and place several small saucers in the freezer.

Place the macerated peaches in a jam pan with the lemon zest and bring to the boil over a high heat. Boil rapidly for 16–18 minutes, stirring intermittently and skimming off scum as you go.

When the bubbles are heavy and start struggling to release, remove
from the heat and start set testing (see page 14) for a loose, soft-set
jam, where the jam slowly drops from your finger.

Once at the desired set, skim off any scum and ladle the hot jam into
hot sterilised jars and seal (see page 15). Store unopened in a cool,
dark place for up to a year. Once opened, keep in the fridge and eat
within 1–2 months.

Greengage and Lemon Thyme Jam

MAKES 5–6 X 230ML/8FL OZ JARS | SUMMER | HIGH PECTIN

Greengages are special as they are quite specific to Western Europe, and I've only discovered them since my time in England. If you can find these on the underripe side, they make for a delicious green-coloured plum jam. Their clingy stones shouldn't deter you from making this jam, as the reward when eating it will diminish any memories of struggles with the prep work.

1.2kg/2lb 11oz greengages,
  pitted weight
90ml/3fl oz water

50ml/2fl oz lemon juice,
  freshly squeezed
4–5 sprigs of lemon thyme
680g/1lb 8oz white sugar

Sterilise your jars and lids (see page 9) and place several small saucers in the freezer.

Cut the pitted greengages into 2–3cm/¾–1¼in cubes and place in a jam pan with the water, lemon juice and the sprigs of lemon thyme (alternatively, pluck off the leaves and add them at the end just before jarring and after skimming off the scum). Soften the fruit over a medium-high heat, stirring intermittently so that it doesn't stick and burn.

Turn up the heat and bring to a rapid boil, stirring through the sugar until completely dissolved. Bring back to the boil, again being vigilant so that it doesn't stick and burn on the bottom of the pan.

After 8–12 minutes, when the bubbles become heavier and struggle to be released, remove from the heat and start set testing (see page 14) for a hard-set jam, with an evident wrinkle on the plate.

Once at the desired set, skim off any scum, remove the lemon thyme stalks (or stir through the leaves, if doing so now) and ladle the hot jam into hot sterilised jars and seal (see page 15). Store unopened in a cool, dark place for up to a year. Once opened, keep in the fridge and eat within 1–2 months.

Red Plum and Hazelnut Jam

MAKES 5–6 X 230ML/8FL OZ JARS | SUMMER | HIGH PECTIN

*Plums are delicious alone, but in my eyes they are destined for jam.
Plums tend to be high in pectin, making them a great candidate for
jam setting. Hazelnuts add a bit of texture to this recipe, but I'm
also a big fan of hazelnuts with tarter, sweeter or creamier pairings
(instead of the traditional chocolate). Envision this jam as a breakfast
treat, dolloped atop some thick Greek yoghurt and toasted buckwheat
groats, topped with torn fresh herbs like basil or mint.*

1.2kg/2lb 11oz red plums (any
    variety), *pitted weight*
90ml/3fl oz water
50ml/2fl oz lemon juice, *freshly
    squeezed*

700g/1lb 9oz white sugar
30g/1oz hazelnuts, *roughly
    chopped*

Sterilise your jars and lids (see page 9) and place several small
saucers in the freezer.

Cut the pitted plums into 2–3cm/¾–1¼in cubes and place in a jam
pan with the water and lemon juice. Soften the fruit into a pulp over
a medium-high heat, stirring often and keeping an eye on it so that
it does not stick and burn.

Turn up the heat and bring to a rapid boil before slowly adding the sugar, stirring until completely dissolved. Bring back to the boil, again being vigilant so that it doesn't stick and burn on the bottom of the pan.

After 5 minutes, add the chopped hazelnuts and continue to boil for 10–12 minutes until the bubbles start to get heavier. Remove from the heat and start set testing (see page 14) for a hard-set jam, with an evident wrinkle on the plate.

Once at the desired set, skim off any scum and ladle the hot jam into hot sterilised jars and seal (see page 15). Store unopened in a cool, dark place for up to a year. Once opened, keep in the fridge and eat within 1–2 months.

Mirabelle and Lavender Preserve

MAKES 4–5 X 230ML/8FL OZ JARS | SUMMER | MEDIUM PECTIN

Originating from France, mirabelle plums have traditionally been grown in the region of Lorraine where they are used for making jam and eau de vie brandy. The trees grow well here in the UK, and mirabelles have grown in popularity over the years. These smaller, oval-shaped plums are bright yellow and much sweeter than a Victoria plum or greengage, making them perfect for a reduced-sugar soft-set jam. This jam is delicious dribbled onto a heavily buttered crumpet and with a hint of lavender; you'll be transported to your favourite province of France at the height of summer.

1kg/2lb 4oz mirabelle plums, *pitted weight*
50ml/2fl oz water

40ml/1 ¼fl oz lemon juice, *freshly squeezed*
500g/1lb 2oz caster sugar
¼ tsp dried lavender petals

Sterilise your jars and lids (see page 9) and place several small saucers in the freezer.

Cut the pitted plums into 2–3cm/¾–1¼in cubes and place in a jam pan with the water and lemon juice. Soften the fruit into a pulp over a medium-high heat, stirring often and keeping an eye on it so that it does not stick and burn.

Turn up the heat and bring to a rapid boil before adding the sugar, stirring until completely dissolved. Bring back to the boil, stirring intermittently and being vigilant so that it doesn't stick and burn on the bottom of the pan.

After 6–8 minutes, when the bubbles start to get heavier and struggle to be released, remove from the heat and start set testing (see page 14) for a soft-set jam, where the jam slowly drops from your finger.

Once at the desired set, skim off any scum, stir through the dried lavender and ladle the hot jam into hot sterilised jars and seal (see page 15). Store unopened in a cool, dark place for up to 6 months. Once opened, keep in the fridge and eat within 3–4 weeks.

Cherry and Cacao Nib Jam

MAKES 4–5 X 230ML/8FL OZ JARS | SUMMER | LOW PECTIN

*When cherries pop up at the corner shop, it's a good indication
(apart from better weather) that it's summer – and the deeper into
summer we go, the sweeter the cherries taste. Since the cherry season
is short, there's a strong need as a preserver to get to work and
jar them up to make the summer last. I like the idea of matching
cherries with an intermittent crunch of cacao nibs – a flavour
reminiscent of a cherry cola.*

1.2kg/2lb 11oz cherries, *pitted
   weight*
50ml/2fl oz lemon juice, *freshly
   squeezed*

600g/1lb 5oz jam sugar
2 tbsp cacao nibs

Place the pitted cherries in a large bowl with the lemon juice and
sugar, cover and macerate in the fridge for 1–2 hours. This will keep
them brighter in colour once made into jam.

Sterilise your jars and lids (see page 9) and place several small
saucers in the freezer.

Pour the maceration into a jam pan and soften the fruit over a
high heat, stirring to dissolve the sugar, then bring it to a vigorous
boil. Stir through the cacao nibs and boil rapidly for 8–10 minutes,
stirring intermittently.

When it starts to look stickier and the bubbles appear heavier, remove from the heat and start set testing (see page 14) for a soft-set jam, where the jam slowly drops from your finger.

Once at the desired set, skim off any scum and ladle into hot sterilised jars and seal (see page 15). Store unopened in a cool, dark place for up to a year. Once opened, keep in the fridge and eat within 1–2 months.

Note: Definitely try making the Cherry and Cacao Nib Pot Brownies (see page 150) using this particular jam. It's a game changer.

Strawberry, Balsamic Vinegar and Black Pepper Jam

MAKES 5–6 X 230ML/8FL OZ JARS | SUMMER | LOW PECTIN

Strawberries are the hardest fruit to get a good jam set without adding the same weight in sugar. They are low in pectin and low in acid, so need a helping hand. This recipe gives you a soft-set jam – one that is gooey, not gelatinous. The balsamic vinegar adds a touch of depth to the strawberries, while the black pepper gives a gentle peppery tickle on the palate. You'll be surprised how delicious this combination is when drizzled onto vanilla or clotted cream ice cream.

1.25kg/2lb 12oz strawberries, hulled
60ml/2¼fl oz water
40ml/1¼fl oz lemon juice, *freshly squeezed*

800g/1lb 12oz jam sugar
1 tbsp balsamic vinegar, *not your 10-year-aged one*
2–3 tsp freshly ground black pepper

Sterilise your jars and lids (see page 9) and place several small saucers in the freezer.

Place the strawberries in a jam pan, cutting the larger ones into halves or thirds and reserving 10–12 of the smallest ones. Add the water and lemon juice and soften the fruit over a high heat for about 10 minutes, stirring often. Gently mash into a pulp, stirring so that it doesn't stick, while skimming off any scum or foam with a spatula.

Bring to a vigorous boil, stir through the sugar until it's completely dissolved, then add the reserved strawberries. Once at a rapid boil, stir intermittently for 10–12 minutes until the bubbles appear heavier. Remove from the heat and start set testing (see page 14) for a soft-set jam, where the jam slowly drops from your finger.

Once at the desired set, allow to settle for 1–2 minutes before skimming off any scum and stirring through the balsamic vinegar and black pepper. Ladle the hot jam into hot sterilised jars and seal (see page 15). Store unopened in a cool, dark place for up to a year. Once opened, keep in the fridge and eat within 1–2 months.

Raspberry and Amaretto Jam

MAKES 5–6 X 230ML/8FL OZ JARS | SUMMER | MEDIUM PECTIN

*Raspberries are an odd one when it comes to jam making. They are
not high in pectin, however they do tend to set well and you don't
need to add any extra pectin or use jam sugar to achieve a good set. I
love the taste of almond and raspberries – I'm a big fan of a Bakewell
tart, so this jam is a flavour homage to that delicious bake.*

1.1kg/2lb 7oz raspberries, *fresh
or frozen*
30ml/1fl oz water, *omit if using
frozen berries*

30ml/1fl oz lemon juice, *freshly
squeezed*
650g/1lb 7oz white sugar
150ml/5fl oz Amaretto, almond
liqueur or almond extract

Sterilise your jars and lids (see page 9) and place several small
saucers in the freezer.

Gently rinse your raspberries, defrost if frozen, and place in a jam
pan with the water (if using) and lemon juice. Soften the fruit over a
medium-high heat for 6–8 minutes until it forms a pulp, stirring so
that it doesn't stick and burn on the bottom of the pan.

Turn the heat up to high and add the sugar when at a vigorous boil,
stirring until completely dissolved. Bring back to the boil for 10–12
minutes, stirring intermittently to stop it catching.

When the bubbles become heavier, stir through the Amaretto and cook for a further 1–2 minutes. Remove from the heat and start set testing (see page 14) for a hard-set jam with an evident wrinkle on the plate.

Once at the desired set, skim off any scum and ladle the hot jam into hot sterilised jars and seal (see page 15). Store unopened in a cool, dark place for up to a year. Once opened, keep in the fridge and eat within 1–2 months.

Note: If you're not a fan of almond flavour then you can easily replace Amaretto with another liqueur. Try Frangelico for a hazelnut flavour or Triple Sec for orange.

Gooseberry and Nigella Seed Jam

MAKES 5–6 X 230ML/8FL OZ JARS | SUMMER | HIGH PECTIN

Instead of turning to your regular store-bought mango chutney to accompany your favourite Indian food, why not try gooseberry jam? The added nigella seeds mimic the flavours you might have running through a curry, yet it still has that sweet stickiness one needs to offset the heat of a vindaloo. Next, you'll be making your own homemade curry and chapati to accompany the jam.

1.2kg/2lb 11oz gooseberries, *fresh or frozen, topped and tailed*

150ml/5fl oz water, *omit if using frozen berries*

40ml/1¼fl oz lemon juice, *freshly squeezed*

650g/1lb 7oz white sugar

1½ tsp nigella seeds

Sterilise your jars and lids (see page 9) and place several small saucers in the freezer.

Rinse the gooseberries, defrost if frozen, and place in a jam pan with the water (if using) and lemon juice. Heat the fruit over a medium-high heat for about 8–10 minutes until it starts breaking down, mashing with a potato masher and stirring as it will want to stick to the bottom of the pan.

Once pulpy, increase the heat to high, bring to a vigorous boil and pour in the sugar, stirring until completely dissolved. Boil for 10–12 minutes, stirring when needed so that it doesn't catch and burn. When the bubbles become heavier, remove from the heat and start set testing (see page 14) for a hard-set jam with an evident wrinkle on the plate.

Once at the desired set, skim off any scum, stir through the nigella seeds and ladle the hot jam into hot sterilised jars and seal (see page 15). Store unopened in a cool, dark place for up to a year. Once opened, keep in the fridge and eat within 1–2 months.

Note: Try and find a local berry farm in your area to 'pick your own'. You'll be surprised how many are scattered around and it makes for a great day out with the kids.

Blackberry and Rosemary Jam

MAKES 5–6 X 230ML/8FL OZ JARS | AUTUMN | HIGH PECTIN

*Pick or find blackberries throughout the autumn months –
although this recipe works well with frozen berries too, so if
you find yourself out of time after a full day's picking, just bag
the berries up, label and date them, and then chuck them in the
freezer until you have a spare day for preserving. The rich, dense
flavour of the blackberries mixed with the rosemary works well
with duck, pheasant or quail. If game isn't your thing, then it is
equally fabulous with lamb, turkey or oven-baked Camembert.*

1.1kg/2lb 7oz blackberries, *fresh
or frozen*
50ml/2fl oz water, *omit if using
frozen berries*

40ml/1¼fl oz lemon juice,
freshly squeezed
3–4 sprigs of rosemary, *leaves
finely chopped*
750g/1lb 10oz white sugar

Sterilise your jars and lids (see page 9) and place several small
saucers in the freezer.

Gently rinse the blackberries and pluck off any husks, defrost if
frozen, and place in a jam pan with the water (if using) and lemon
juice – reserving 10–15 whole berries here if you like a chunkier jam.
Pulp the berries over a high heat for 5–8 minutes, stirring so that
they don't stick to the bottom of the pan.

Mix the rosemary through the sugar and pour into the pan, stirring until the sugar has completely dissolved. Bring back to a vigorous boil, then add any reserved berries and stir intermittently for 8–10 minutes. When the bubbles become heavier, remove from the heat and start set testing (see page 14) for a hard-set jam with an evident wrinkle on the plate.

Once at the desired set, skim off any scum and ladle the hot jam into hot sterilised jars and seal (see page 15). Store unopened in a cool, dark place for up to a year. Once opened, keep in the fridge and eat within 1–2 months.

Vermouth Poached Pear Jam

MAKES 4–5 X 230ML/8FL OZ JARS

AUTUMN-WINTER | LOW PECTIN

Poached pears make a delicious dessert – serve them with some clotted cream, ice cream or homemade vanilla custard and you really can't go wrong. Dollop this jam onto yoghurt and fresh fruit for breakfast, mix it with fresh pears to make individual crumble pots, or try atop ricotta, stracciatella or burrata crostini with sprigs of marjoram or lemon thyme.

250ml/9fl oz sweet vermouth
   or white wine

1 cinnamon stick

4 green cardamom pods, *gently crushed*

2–3 slices of fresh ginger

¼ tsp black peppercorns

4 strips of pared lemon peel, *unwaxed*

2 tbsp golden granulated sugar

1kg/2lb 4oz firm pears, *peeled and cored*

60ml/2¼fl oz lemon juice, *freshly squeezed*

850g/1lb 14oz jam sugar

Sterilise your jars and lids (see page 9) and place several small saucers in the freezer.

Make a poaching liquor by infusing the vermouth with the spices, lemon peel and golden granulated sugar in a large pan over a high heat for 5 minutes. Roughly chop three-quarters of the pears, add to the pan and gently simmer for a further 5–6 minutes. Leave to cool and sit for at least 2 hours, then strain, discarding any spices and the poaching liquor. Blitz the poached pears into a pulp in a food processor.

Cut the remaining pears into 1cm/½in cubes. Place the pulped pear in a large jam pan with the lemon juice and bring to the boil. Stir through the sugar until completely dissolved, then add the pear cubes. Turn up the heat and bring to a vigorous boil for 12–15 minutes, stirring intermittently so that the jam doesn't stick and burn. When the bubbles become heavier, remove from the heat and start set testing (see page 14) for a soft-set jam, where the jam slowly drops from your finger.

Once at the desired set, skim off any scum and ladle the hot jam into hot sterilised jars and seal (see page 15). Store unopened in a cool, dark place for up to a year. Once opened, keep in the fridge and eat within 1–2 months.

Rhubarb and Rose Jam

MAKES 6–7 X 230ML/8FL OZ JARS

SUMMER (FIELD), WINTER (FORCED) | LOW PECTIN

Rhubarb, although officially a vegetable, makes for great jam. In the winter, forced rhubarb, predominately from the 'Rhubarb Triangle' in West Yorkshire, is grown in darkened barns and harvested by candlelight. Starving it of light creates the wonderful pink hue we associate with rhubarb – a gorgeous colour for jam. Use field rhubarb if making this jam in the spring or summer – but note that the photosynthesis process in this field variety gives it a green tint, so you won't get the rose hues to match the rose scent in this jam.

1.3kg/3lb forced or field rhubarb, *cut into 1–2cm/ ½–¾in cubes*
100ml/3½fl oz water
60ml/2¼fl oz lemon juice, *freshly squeezed*

700g/1lb 9oz jam sugar
1 tbsp rose water or ½ tsp rose extract
1 tbsp dried rose petals

Sterilise your jars and lids (see page 9) and place several small saucers in the freezer.

Place the prepared rhubarb in a jam pan with the water and lemon juice. Soften over a medium heat for 6–8 minutes, stirring often so that it doesn't stick and burn on the bottom of the pan.

When it becomes a pulp, bring to a rapid boil over the highest heat and stir through the sugar until it has completely dissolved. Return to a vigorous boil for 8–10 minutes, stirring intermittently. When the bubbles start to get heavier, remove from the heat and start set testing (see page 14) for a soft-set jam, where the jam slowly drops from your finger.

Once at the desired set, carefully skim off any scum, stir through the rose water and petals and ladle the hot jam into hot sterilised jars and seal (see page 15). Store unopened in a cool, dark place for up to a year. Once opened, keep in the fridge and eat within 1–2 months.

Note: Rose can be an overpowering flavour, but not as 'perfumy' as you'd think if used wisely. Add a little at a time to suit your taste and make a note of how much you can handle.

Blackcurrant and Orange Jelly

MAKES 3–4 X 230ML/8FL OZ JARS | SUMMER | HIGH PECTIN

Blackcurrants have a short season – July to August in the UK – and are mainly commercially grown for the juicing industry, so they can be hard to buy unless farmers have a larger production quantity than industries require. However, you can grow your own: even if you don't have a garden and are short of space, just pot them in containers on a terrace or in a sunny kitchen. Blackcurrants are rich in vitamin C and high in pectin, and therefore make perfect jelly and jam.

1.2kg/2lb 11oz blackcurrants
750ml/1⅓ pints water
350–400g/12–14oz white sugar

100ml/3½fl oz orange juice, *freshly squeezed, strained*
1 orange, *finely zested*

Pluck the currants from the stalks and rinse, then place them in a large pot or pan with the water and bring to a simmer over a medium heat for 20 minutes. Gently crush the softened berries, breaking them up, but don't over-mash.

Strain through a large square of muslin tied up by all corners and suspended over a bowl, or use a jelly bag. Leave for up to 8 hours or overnight, without being tempted to squeeze the bag.

The next day, sterilise your jars and lids (see page 9) and place several small saucers in the freezer.

Measure out the liquid: for every 200ml/7fl oz of liquid, weigh out 160g/5¾oz of sugar. Pour the blackcurrant liquid into a jam pan with the orange juice and zest and bring to a rapid boil over the highest heat, then stir through the sugar until completely dissolved.

When the jelly reaches 104°C/219°F on a sugar thermometer, or when it has been at a rapid boil for 8–10 minutes, remove from the heat and start set testing (see page 14) for a hard set. If there isn't an evident wrinkle on the plate, return to the heat and keep testing every minute until there is.

Once at the desired set, carefully skim off any scum and quickly ladle the hot jelly into hot sterilised jars and seal (see page 15). Store unopened in a cool, dark place for up to a year. Once opened, keep in the fridge and eat within 3–4 months.

Apple and Cinnamon Jelly

MAKES 4–5 X 230ML/8FL OZ JARS | SUMMER–WINTER | HIGH PECTIN

*I like to use Bramley apples for this – great-tasting cooking
apples that are high in pectin to help get a good jelly set. If
you have access to crab apples, these also work well. Different
apples have different pectin levels, so if using your favourite
variety be aware of different timings for that perfect set.*

1.5kg/3lb 5oz Bramley apples,
  *unwaxed or scrubbed and
  roughly chopped (with skins,
  pips and cores)*
1.5 litres/2¾ pints water
700–750g/1lb 9oz–1lb 10oz
  white sugar

¼ tsp ground cinnamon
30ml/1fl oz lemon juice, *freshly
  squeezed, strained*
2 small cinnamon sticks, *cut
  into halves*

Place the prepared apples in a large pot or pan with the water and
bring to a simmer over a medium heat. After 20 minutes, gently
crush the softened apples with a wooden spoon, without over-
mashing.

Strain through a large square of muslin tied up by all corners and
suspended over a bowl, or use a jelly bag. Leave for up to 8 hours or
overnight, without being tempted to squeeze the bag.

The next day, sterilise your jars and lids (see page 9) and place several small saucers in the freezer.

Measure out the liquid; for every 200ml/7fl oz of liquid, weigh out 140g/5oz of sugar. Mix the ground cinnamon through the sugar. Pour the apple liquid into a jam pan with the lemon juice and bring to a rapid boil over the highest heat, then stir through the sugar until completely dissolved.

When the jelly reaches 104°C/219°F on a sugar thermometer, or when it's been at a vigorous boil for 5–6 minutes, remove from the heat and start set testing (see page 14) for a hard set. If there isn't an evident wrinkle on the plate, return to the heat and keep testing every minute until there is.

Once at the desired set, skim off any scum and set up your hot sterilised jars with half a cinnamon stick in each. Quickly ladle in the hot jelly and seal (see page 15). Store unopened in a cool, dark place for up to a year. Once opened, keep in the fridge and eat within 3–4 months.

Low Peel Orange and Fennel Seed Marmalade

MAKES 4–5 X 230ML/8FL OZ JARS | AUTUMN–WINTER | HIGH PECTIN

When life gives you oranges, make marmalade. There are several different ways to make marmalade, but this one gives you a low-peel version, as not everyone is a fan of that bitter skin in their morning spread. I've included fennel seeds in this recipe, as I love matching orange with aniseed flavours like fennel.

1.4kg/3lb 3oz thin-skinned oranges, *unwaxed or scrubbed*
750ml/1¼ pints water
40ml/1¼fl oz lemon juice, *freshly squeezed*

850g/1lb 14oz white sugar or preserving sugar
2 tsp fennel seeds

Sterilise your jars and lids (see page 9) and place several small saucers in the freezer.

Cut 2 of the oranges in half and juice into the jam pan. Scrape out and discard the remaining flesh and white pith. Slice these skins into very fine (1mm) thin strips.

Using a sharp knife, slice off all the skin and pith of the remaining oranges, and chop the flesh into 1cm chunks. Place in your jam pan with the juice collected on your chopping board, discarding any pips. Add the water and lemon juice, bring to the boil and cook for 20 minutes, stirring intermittently.

Pour in the sugar, stirring until it dissolves completely. Bring back to a rapid boil over the highest heat for 18–20 minutes, stirring only when needed. Remove from the heat and start set testing (see page 14) for a hard-set jam. If there isn't an evident wrinkle on the plate, return to the heat and keep testing every minute until there is.

Once at the desired set, skim off any scum and stir through the fennel seeds, then ladle the marmalade into hot sterilised jars and seal (see page 15). Store unopened in a cool, dark place for up to a year. Once opened, keep in the fridge and eat within 3–4 months.

Note: If you like more peel in your marmalades, simply follow the same method but add two more oranges to the first part of the instructions.

Lemon and Chamomile Marmalade

MAKES 4–5 X 230ML/8FL OZ JARS | AUTUMN–WINTER | HIGH PECTIN

When pairing citrus flavours as tart as lemon, you want to even them out with something mellow. Chamomile tea, known for its calming properties, makes for the perfect balance here.

2 tbsp dried chamomile buds or 3 chamomile teabags, *split*
800ml/1⅓ pints water, *boiled*

1kg/2lb 4oz thin-skinned lemons, *unwaxed or scrubbed*
700g/1lb 9oz white sugar or preserving sugar

Sterilise your jars and lids (see page 9) and place several small saucers in the freezer.

Add the chamomile to the boiled water and brew for 5 minutes.

Squeeze the juice of two of the lemons into a jam pan. Carefully cut the skin off half of the lemons, discard the skin and chop the flesh into 1cm chunks. Cut the remaining lemons in half lengthways and finely slice into 1mm semicircles, then add to the pan with the juice collected on your chopping board, discarding as many pips as you can.

Add the chamomile tea to the lemons and bring to the boil over a medium-high heat, stirring intermittently for 12–15 minutes to soften. Stir through the sugar until it has completely dissolved and bring back to a rapid boil over the highest heat for 8–12 minutes, stirring only when needed.

Remove from the heat and start set testing (see page 14) for a hard-set jam. If there isn't an evident wrinkle on the plate, return to the heat and keep testing every minute until there is.

Once at the desired set, skim off any scum, then ladle the marmalade into hot sterilised jars and seal (see page 15). Store unopened in a cool, dark place for up to a year. Once opened, keep in the fridge and eat within 3–4 months.

Ruby Grapefruit Aperol Spritz Marmalade

MAKES 5–6 X 230ML/8FL OZ JARS

AUTUMN–WINTER | MEDIUM PECTIN

Adding alcohol to jam must be one of my favourite ways to make jam with a twist. It's like creating cocktails – another thing I like to do, as well as drinking them! This is my take on bringing those summer vibes to a winter fruit.

1.3kg/3lb ruby grapefruit,
 unwaxed or scrubbed
800ml/1⅓ pints water
40ml/1¼fl oz lemon juice,
 freshly squeezed

900g white sugar or preserving
 sugar
60ml/2¼fl oz Aperol
75ml/2½fl oz sparkling wine,
 prosecco or cava

Sterilise your jars and lids (see page 9) and place several small saucers in the freezer.

With a sharp knife, cut off the skins of the grapefruit and discard half the peel. Scrape off the white pith from the peel with a teaspoon or a sharp paring knife. Slice the prepared peel into very fine (1mm) strips. Dice the grapefruit flesh into 1cm chunks, removing as much of the pips and membrane as you can. Place in a jam pan with any juice on the chopping board, the peel strips, water and lemon juice.

Bring to the boil over a medium-high heat for about 10–15 minutes, stirring intermittently to soften. Stir through the sugar until it dissolves completely and bring back to a rapid boil over the highest heat for 15–18 minutes, stirring only when needed.

Remove from the heat and start set testing (see page 14) for a hard-set jam. If there isn't an evident wrinkle on the plate, return to the heat and keep testing every minute until there is.

Once at the desired set, pour in the Aperol and sparkling wine and boil for a further 3 minutes.

Take off the heat and allow to settle for 3 minutes, then ladle into hot sterilised jars and seal (see page 15). Store unopened in a cool, dark place for up to a year. Once opened, keep in the fridge and eat within 3–4 months.

Spiced Carrot Marmalade

MAKES 4–5 X 230ML/8FL OZ JARS

ALL SEASONS | ORANGES MODERATE IN PECTIN

*A marmalade for those who claim they don't like marmalade,
so don't be fooled; this is not a bitter version. Eat with
cheese, or in a ham baguette filled with rocket and cheese,
and try it in desserts too, such as meringues topped with
whipped cream, or as the base of steamed puddings.*

850g/1lb 14oz oranges,
   unwaxed or scrubbed
600g/1lb 5oz carrots, *peeled
   and grated*
680g/1lb 8oz white sugar
⅛ tsp ground cinnamon

4 green cardamom pods,
   gently crushed
2 star anise
420ml/15fl oz water
50ml/2fl oz lemon juice, *freshly
   squeezed*

With a sharp knife, cut off the skins of the oranges and discard half
of the peel. Scrape off the white pith using a teaspoon or a very
sharp paring knife. Slice the prepared peel into very fine (1mm)
strips. Dice the orange flesh into 1cm/½in chunks, removing as
much of the pips and membrane as you can. Place in a large bowl
with any juice from the chopping board and the grated carrots. Mix
through the sugar, cinnamon, cardamom and star anise, cover and
leave to macerate in the fridge for 6–8 hours or overnight.

The next day, sterilise your jars and lids (see page 9) and place several small saucers in the freezer. Place the carrot mixture in a jam pan with the water and lemon juice, then bring to a rapid boil over a medium-high heat, stirring intermittently, for 25–35 minutes or until the liquid has reduced to a thicker, stickier jammy consistency.

Once at the desired set, pick out the spices and ladle the marmalade into hot sterilised jars (see page 15), using a teaspoon to push out any trapped air bubbles. Seal and store, unopened, in a cool, dark place for up to 8–10 months. Once opened, keep in the fridge and eat within 3–4 months.

Courgette, Lemon and Thyme Marmalade

MAKES 5–6 X 230ML/8FL OZ JARS

SUMMER | LEMONS HIGH IN PECTIN

Got a glut of courgettes? This is a recurring story among many people who reach out to me – either that or they have let them grow until they start resembling marrows. But have no fear: this recipe is the perfect solution to this common problem.

600g/1lb 5oz thin-skinned lemons, *unwaxed or scrubbed*
500ml/18fl oz water
1kg /2lb 4oz courgettes, *peeled*

½ tsp cracked black pepper
5–6 sprigs of thyme
750g/1lb 10oz jam sugar

Sterilise your jars and lids (see page 9) and place several small saucers in the freezer.

Carefully cut off the skin of two-thirds of the lemons and discard the peel. Dice the remaining flesh into 1cm/½in chunks, discarding as much pith, pips and membrane as you can. Cut the remaining lemons in half lengthways and finely slice into 1mm semicircles. Add all the prepared lemon to a large saucepan with the juice collected from the chopping board and the water. Bring to the boil, turn down the heat and simmer for 15–20 minutes, stirring intermittently.

Meanwhile, chop the courgettes into 1cm/½in cubes, add them to a jam pan with 6–8 tablespoons of the lemon cooking liquor, the pepper and thyme, and sauté over a medium heat for 8–10 minutes until the juices have disappeared.

Add the lemon mixture to the courgettes, bring to a rapid boil over the highest heat, then stir through the sugar until it dissolves completely. Bring back to a rapid boil for 8–10 minutes, stirring only when needed.

Remove from the heat and start set testing (see page 14) for a hard-set jam. If there isn't an evident wrinkle on the plate, return to the heat and keep testing every minute until there is.

Once ready, remove the thyme sprigs, add one to each hot sterilised jar and ladle in the jam (see page 15), using a teaspoon to push out any trapped air bubbles. Seal and store, unopened, in a cool, dark place for up to a year. Once opened, keep in the fridge and eat within 3–4 months.

Grilled Red Pepper and Chilli Jam

MAKES 2–3 X 230ML/8FL OZ JARS | SUMMER | LOW PECTIN

This is a recipe my mum put me on to during a recent summer visit back home to New Zealand. It is so good that she continuously has it made up and ready for any impromptu visit from a friend. It's best served with cheese, crackers and wine, but I'm sure you'll find lots of other scrumptious uses for it.

2 large red peppers
120g/4¼oz long red chillies
3 cloves garlic, *peeled*
1 small red onion, *peeled*
50g/1¾oz fresh ginger, *peeled and finely grated*

1 lime, *grated zest and juice*
260g/9¼oz caster sugar
140ml/4½fl oz white wine vinegar or distilled white vinegar

Preheat the oven to 200°C/190°C fan/gas 6.

Cut the peppers in half lengthways, remove the seeds, place on a baking sheet or roasting tin and roast them for 20–25 minutes, until they're softened and the skins can be easily removed. Turn the oven down to 100°C/90°C fan/gas ¼ and sterilise your jars and lids (see page 9).

Meanwhile, cut the chillies lengthways, deseed (or leave the seeds in for a hotter version) and roughly chop. Put into a food processor with the peeled peppers and blitz for a few pulses.

Roughly chop the garlic and onion and add to the pepper/chilli mixture with the ginger, lime zest and juice. Blitz for a few more pulses until smooth and place in a medium pan over a low heat. Stir through the sugar until completely dissolved before adding the vinegar.

Bring to a rapid boil and cook, stirring intermittently, for 25–35 minutes or until thickened to a sticky jam-like consistency.

Once ready, ladle into hot sterilised jars (see page 15), using a teaspoon to push out any trapped air bubbles. Seal and store, unopened, in a cool, dark place for up to 6–8 months. Once opened, keep in the fridge and eat within 3–4 weeks.

Chapter 2

Pick to Preserve

You'll be surprised by how much nature has to contribute to your preserving practice, from plums and rowans in local streets and parks to the herbs and flowers in your own garden – not to mention the wilder jewels found amongst the hedgerows on pathways and national trails.

People have gathered food from nature for hundreds of thousands of years, mostly as a means of survival in the nomadic hunter-gatherer times. Now, as we crave less exposure to the chemicals from mass food production, we are rediscovering a need to be closer to nature, knowing how our food is grown and what its carbon footprint is, and so foraging is making a proud comeback.

Many of you may already be out there in the foraging playground using bramble bushes, wild garlic, stinging nettles and elderflowers. Wild ingredients are frequently seen on menus these days in many fine establishments. But there is a lot more out there to discover, the hedgerow being one of my favourites, and I'd like this next chapter to form a 'beginner's guide' that introduces you to some other ingredients to add to your jammy repertoire. Plus, it's fun to get outside, breathe in fresh air, follow the seasons and learn a little more about the plants around us.

Pick as much as you like from your own garden. However, please follow a few simple rules when you are out in the countryside or parks to make your gathering fun, safe and sustainable for everyone.

• Always use a number of reliable wild food identification guides to be sure about what you are picking and eating, and be aware that some plants have inedible and sometimes poisonous look-alikes. There are lots of great foraging books and websites that specifically identify the characteristics of what you have picked: try wildfooduk.com or britishlocalfood.com

• Only pick what you need and what's plentiful. Over-picking can damage plants and impact the next year's growth, so only pick when it's in abundance and it doesn't make a dent for the next person who comes along to harvest. It's against the law to uproot a plant anywhere in Britain, unless you are on private land and have the landowner's permission. Some rare plants are also protected by law from any kind of picking, though few of these bear fruit used for jams.

• Respect the land. Stick to public rights of way and don't trespass onto private property unless you have permission. A lot of other land is open access for recreation in the UK but this may not include the right to forage. Some places have signs up with local bylaws or foraging guides to help – pay attention to these. Minimise trampling through growth to get to something else, leave no trace behind, and take care of habitats and the wildlife within them. It's best not to forage on Sites of Special Scientific Interest (SSSIs) – ASSIs in Northern Ireland – or National Nature Reserves (NNR) as they are likely to have bylaws preventing the picking of plants.

- Avoid polluted areas that might be sprayed with pesticides, fertilisers and herbicides. Do your homework to find out if there are any polluted water sources that might taint plants growing nearby. Use your instincts when it comes to low-growing plants on streets, roadsides, pathways or public walkways where dogs might like to spray.

- Take proper tools like a sharp knife, scissors, garden pruners or secateurs. This causes less damage to the plants you are harvesting – you don't want to pull up any roots or snap any branches – and gives them the best chance to regrow or fruit well the following year. Just cut off leaves, berries and flowers (and stems if using herbs).

- Prep all foraged matter (berries, flowers, leaves, etc.) by washing thoroughly first. Pick out any unwanted bugs, leaves, stalks, stems or browned/rotting bits. Take the time to pluck berries off their stems or stalks and use only the fruit when cooking.

NOTE:
While the publishers and I have taken every care in the preparation of this book, neither I, the National Trust or HarperCollins can accept any responsibility or liability for the end results of the recipes featured. Be cautious when foraging and always check multiple sources that you have picked correctly before making and consuming your harvest. Also, avoid any unfamiliar ingredients if you have any allergies, medical conditions, are pregnant or breastfeeding – just in case something doesn't agree with you.

Spruce Needle Jelly

MAKES 3–4 X 230ML/8FL OZ JARS | SPRING | LOW PECTIN

Although conifer pines are evergreen, it's the new spring needle tips of spruce trees that you need for this recipe. The piney, citrus flavour works well in both savoury and sweet dishes; I like to use this jelly as a substitute for mint jelly when eating my Sunday roast lamb, but try it in desserts and cocktails alike.

1kg/2lb 4oz Bramley or crab apples, *unwaxed or scrubbed and roughly chopped (skins, pips and cores)*
1.2 litres/2 pints water
3 strips of pared lemon peel, *unwaxed*

400g/14oz spruce tips, *rinsed*
30ml/1fl oz lemon juice, *freshly squeezed, strained*
550–650g/1lb 4oz–1lb 7oz white sugar

Place the prepped apples in a large pot or pan with the water, lemon peel and spruce tips, reserving 4–5 for later. Bring to a simmer over a medium heat for about 25 minutes, gently crushing the apples without over-mashing.

Strain through a large square of muslin tied up by all corners and suspended over a bowl, or use a jelly bag. Leave for up to 8 hours or overnight, without being tempted to squeeze the bag.

The next day, sterilise your jars and lids (see page 9) and place several small saucers in the freezer.

Measure out the apple/spruce liquid; for every 200ml/7fl oz of liquid, weigh out 150g/5½oz of sugar. Pour the liquid into a jam pan with the lemon juice and bring to a rapid boil over the highest heat, then stir through the sugar until completely dissolved.

When the jelly reaches 104°C/219°F on a sugar thermometer, or when it's been at a vigorous boil for at least 5–6 minutes, remove from the heat and start set testing (see page 14) for a hard set. If there isn't an evident wrinkle on the plate, return to the heat and keep testing every minute until there is.

Roughly chop the remaining spruce tips and, once at the desired set, carefully skim off any scum, stir through the spruce and quickly ladle into hot sterilised jars and seal (see page 15). Store unopened in a cool, dark place for up to a year. Once opened, keep in the fridge and eat within 3–4 months.

Mahonia (Oregon Grape) and Ginger Jelly

MAKES 4–5 X 230ML/8FL OZ JARS

LATE SPRING–SUMMER | HIGH PECTIN

Mahonia berries are very common, and you will see them everywhere in hedgerows as you walk around your neighbourhood. The berries drape down in a cluster, mimicking deep purple grapes – hence their other name, 'Oregon grape'. Pick with caution: the leaves bear spikes, so snip them off at the top of the cluster to avoid getting pricked. Having a woody taste, they're not common in many hedgerow recipes but when matched with ginger they become a strong contender for anyone's condiment collection.

750g/1lb 10oz mahonia berries, *rinsed and plucked from stalks*
600g/1lb 5oz Bramley apples, *unwaxed or scrubbed and roughly chopped (with skins, pips and cores)*
1.4 litres/2½ pints water

30ml/1fl oz lemon juice, *freshly squeezed, strained*
15g/½oz knob of stem ginger, *peeled and grated*
700–800g/1lb 9oz–1lb 12oz white sugar

Place the prepped berries and apples in a large pot or pan with the water and bring to a simmer over a medium heat for 20–25 minutes, gently crushing the softened berries without over-mashing.

Strain through a large square of muslin tied up by all corners and suspended over a bowl, or use a jelly bag. Leave for up to 8 hours or overnight, without being tempted to squeeze the bag.

The next day, sterilise your jars and lids (see page 9) and place several small saucers in the freezer.

Measure out the berry/apple liquid; for every 200ml/7fl oz of liquid, weigh out 160g/5¾oz of sugar. Pour the liquid into a jam pan with the lemon juice and grated ginger, bring to a rapid boil over the highest heat, then stir through the sugar until completely dissolved.

When the jelly reaches 104°C/219°F on a sugar thermometer, or when it's been at a vigorous boil for at least 5–6 minutes, remove from the heat and start set testing (see page 14) for a hard-set jam. If there isn't an evident wrinkle on the plate, return to the heat and keep testing every minute until there is.

Once at the desired set, carefully skim off any scum with a spatula and quickly ladle into hot sterilised jars and seal (see page 15). Store unopened in a cool, dark place for up to a year. Once opened, keep in the fridge and eat within 3–4 months.

Wild (Sour) Cherry and Garden Rose Jam

MAKES 3–4 X 230ML/8FL OZ JARS | SUMMER | LOW PECTIN

Wild cherries grow in clusters and tend to be smaller and much more sour than the common variety, so making a jam with them is preferable to eating these flirtatious fruits straight from the tree. They are so flirtatious, in fact, that you may find yourself competing with the birds to enjoy their delights. If you choose to substitute the wild variety for sweeter store-bought cherries, make sure to add less sugar and more lemon juice for a more balanced flavour.

2–4 fragrant garden roses, *depending on size*
900g/2lb wild cherries, *pitted weight*

650g/1lb 7oz jam sugar
40ml/1¼fl oz lemon juice, *freshly squeezed*
1–2 tbsp rose water *(optional)*

Pick the most scented of your garden roses and very gently rinse and pluck off the petals. Place in a large bowl with the pitted cherries and gently mix in the sugar and lemon juice. Cover and macerate in the fridge for 6–8 hours.

Sterilise your jars and lids (see page 9) and place several small saucers in the freezer.

Pour the cherry maceration into a jam pan and soften the fruit over a high heat, stirring to dissolve the sugar. Bring to a vigorous boil and boil for 6–8 minutes, stirring only when needed. When the bubbles become heavier, remove from the heat and start to set test (see page 14) for a soft-set jam, where the jam slowly drops from your finger.

Once at the desired set, skim off any scum and taste to decide if you want a stronger rose flavour; if so, stir through rose water to your desired strength. Ladle the jam into hot sterilised jars and seal (see page 15). Store unopened in a cool, dark place for up to 8–10 months. Once opened, keep in the fridge and eat within 1–2 months.

Redcurrant and Lemon Verbena Jelly

MAKES 4–5 X 230ML/8FL OZ JARS | SUMMER | HIGH PECTIN

*Redcurrants do grow wild in the UK, but they are more abundant
if you take the plunge and grow them yourself in your garden or
allotment. They do well in almost any situation and like part-shade,
so try growing potted on a balcony. Closely related to the gooseberry,
they are high in pectin so perfect for jelly setting. I can't resist their
ruby-red appearance; they're like jewels begging to be plucked and
made into a crystal-clear red jelly. I like to add lemon verbena, as
it brings a citrusy boost to the redcurrants. Try growing your own
lemon verbena too, in a sunny spot on your balcony or kitchen sill.*

1.3kg/3lb redcurrants, *rinsed
and plucked from stalks/leaves*
800ml/1⅓ pints water
6–8 sprigs of fresh lemon
verbena or 3g dried lemon
verbena leaves/tea

700–750g/1lb 9oz–1lb 10oz
white sugar
40ml/1¼fl oz lemon juice,
freshly squeezed, strained

Place the prepped currants in a large pot or pan with the water and
lemon verbena and bring to the boil over a medium heat. Simmer
for about 20–25 minutes, then gently crush without over-mashing.

Strain through a large square of muslin tied up by all corners and
suspended over a bowl, or use a jelly bag. Leave for up to 8 hours or
overnight, without being tempted to squeeze the bag.

The next day, sterilise your jars and lids (see page 9) and place several small saucers in the freezer.

Measure out the redcurrant liquid; for every 200ml/7fl oz of liquid, weigh out 150g/5½oz of sugar. Pour the liquid into a jam pan with the lemon juice and bring to a rapid boil over the highest heat, then stir through the sugar until completely dissolved.

When the jelly reaches 104°C/219°F on a sugar thermometer, or when it's been at a vigorous boil for at least 5–6 minutes, remove from the heat and start set testing (see page 14) for a hard-set jam. If there isn't an evident wrinkle on the plate, return to the heat and keep testing every minute until there is.

Once at the desired set, carefully skim off any scum with a spatula and quickly ladle into hot sterilised jars and seal (see page 15). Store unopened in a cool, dark place for up to a year. Once opened, keep in the fridge and eat within 3–4 months.

Wild Strawberry and Roast Angelica Compote

MAKES APPROX. 500G/1LB 2OZ | SUMMER | LOW PECTIN

Although you'd believe wild strawberries are only found in the wild, they can actually be gathered by city dwellers and seasoned foragers alike. Look out for a patch in urban nooks and crannies, growing through fences backed onto hedges, parks, fields, woods, meadows or railways. Angelica can be grown in your garden as well as foraged in the wild – use the stems as you might use rhubarb in recipes.
This recipe is a small-yield compote – collecting a lot of wild strawberries can be challenging – so do double the quantities if using home-grown strawberries or store-bought varieties, and add a little more time to your cooking.

200g/7oz wild strawberries, *hulled*
180g/6oz golden caster sugar
40ml/1¼fl oz water
½ lemon, *finely zested*
1 star anise

200g/7oz wild or garden angelica, *stalks or stems (or 200g fennel)*
20ml/¾fl oz lemon juice, *freshly squeezed*

Wash the hulled strawberries and pat dry, then place them in a bowl with 150g/5½oz of the sugar, cover and macerate in the fridge for 1–2 hours.

Preheat the oven to 180°C/170°C fan/gas 4 and line a baking sheet with non-stick baking paper.

Pour the water into a medium saucepan, stir in the remaining sugar, the lemon zest and star anise and bring to the boil. Wash and cut the angelica stems into 2cm/¾in lengths (or finely chop the fennel if using instead), add to the sugar syrup and simmer for 4–5 minutes until the angelica is soft to the touch. Fish out the angelica, keeping the syrup aside, and place on the prepared baking sheet. Bake in the middle of the oven for 10–12 minutes.

Add the macerated strawberries to the sugar syrup with the lemon juice. Bring to the boil, then stir through the roast angelica. Boil for about 6–8 minutes, stirring often so the compote doesn't stick, and starts to thicken up.

Remove from the heat and pour into a Tupperware container, or a bowl you can cover, and leave to cool. Store in the fridge for up to 2 weeks or the freezer for up to 6 months. Defrost in the fridge overnight if frozen. Enjoy atop yoghurt or toasted granola.

Rowan Berry and Elderflower Jelly

MAKES 5–6 X 230ML/8FL OZ JARS

SUMMER–EARLY AUTUMN | HIGH PECTIN

Rowan trees are found throughout the British Isles, making them easy to forage. The rowan bloom is not dissimilar to an elderflower; the berries come in clusters, much like the elderberry, but the berries are larger. The distinguishing feature is their colour – elderberries are black, whereas rowan berries range from yellowy orange to a bright lipstick red.

1kg/2lb 4oz rowan berries, *rinsed and plucked from stalks/leaves*

500g/1lb 2oz Bramley or crab apples, *unwaxed or scrubbed and roughly chopped (with skins, pips and cores)*

1.2 litres/2 pints water

½ lemon

40ml/1¼fl oz lemon juice, *freshly squeezed, strained*

800–850g/1lb 12oz–1lb 14oz white sugar

100ml/3½fl oz elderflower cordial or syrup

Place the prepped rowan berries and apples in a large pot or pan with the water and lemon half. Bring to a simmer over a medium heat for 20–25 minutes, gently crushing without over-mashing.

Strain through a large square of muslin tied up by all corners and suspended over a bowl, or use a jelly bag. Leave for up to 8 hours or overnight, without being tempted to squeeze the bag.

The next day, sterilise your jars and lids (see page 9) and place several small saucers in the freezer. Measure out the rowan berry/apple liquid; for every 200ml/7fl oz of liquid, weigh out 160g/5¾oz of sugar. Pour the liquid into a jam pan with the lemon juice and bring to a rapid boil over the highest heat, then stir through the sugar until completely dissolved.

When the jelly reaches 104°C/219°F on a sugar thermometer, or when it's been at a vigorous boil for at least 8–10 minutes, remove from the heat and start set testing (see page 14) for a hard-set jam. If there isn't an evident wrinkle on the plate, return to the heat and keep testing every minute until there is.

Once at the desired set, carefully skim off any scum with a spatula and stir through the elderflower cordial. Quickly ladle into hot sterilised jars and seal (see page 15). Store unopened in a cool, dark place for up to a year. Once opened, keep in the fridge and eat within 3–4 months.

Elderberry, Apple and Garden Thyme Jelly

MAKES 4–5 X 230ML/8FL OZ JARS | LATE SUMMER | LOW PECTIN

If you haven't managed to make your annual elderflower cordial this year and the usual cluster of flowers have turned into red-stemmed black berries on your favourite elder tree, then try elderberry jelly instead – you may be converted. As elderberries are low in pectin, I use cooking apples to stabilise the jelly.

18–20 elderberry heads, *rinsed and plucked from stalks/leaves*
800g/1lb 12oz Bramley or crab apples, *unwaxed or scrubbed and roughly chopped (with skins, pips and cores)*
1 litre/1¾ pints water

50ml/2fl oz lemon juice, *freshly squeezed, strained*
750–800g/1lb 10z–1lb 12oz white sugar
3 sprigs of garden thyme, *leaves picked*

Place the prepped elderberries and apples in a large pan or pot and cover with the water. Bring to a simmer over a medium heat for 20–25 minutes, gently crushing without over-mashing.

Strain through a large square of muslin tied up by all corners and suspended over a bowl, or use a jelly bag. Leave for up to 8 hours or overnight, without being tempted to squeeze the bag.

The next day, sterilise your jars and lids (see page 9) and place several small saucers in the freezer.

Measure out the elderberry/apple liquid; for every 200ml/7fl oz of liquid, weigh out 180g/6oz of sugar. Pour the liquid into a jam pan with the lemon juice and bring to a rapid boil over the highest heat, then stir through the sugar until completely dissolved.

When the jelly reaches 104°C/219°F on a sugar thermometer, or when it's been at a vigorous boil for at least 5-6 minutes, remove from the heat and start set testing (see page 14) for a hard-set jam. If there isn't an evident wrinkle on the plate, return to the heat and keep testing every minute until there is.

Once at the desired set, skim off any scum and stir through the thyme leaves. Quickly ladle into hot sterilised jars and seal (see page 15). Store unopened in a cool, dark place for up to a year. Once opened, keep in the fridge and eat within 3-4 months.

Sage Cobnut Salted Caramel

MAKES 3–4 X 230ML/8FL OZ JARS | LATE SUMMER | LOW PECTIN

*Cobnuts are young, green, husky hazelnuts found on hazel trees
and traditionally grown around Kent. If you have come too late in
the season to use them as cobnuts, then this recipe works equally
well with the now 'turned' hazelnuts. You can buy cobnuts in stores
everywhere these days, but if all else fails just use store-bought
hazelnuts instead. This is not strictly a jam or jelly – but it makes an
incredibly tasty, spreadable treat.*

300g/10½oz cobnuts, *husks and
shells removed (850g/1lb 14oz
with husks/680g/1lb 8oz with
shells)*
3–4 sage leaves
1 tsp sea salt

100–120ml/3½–4fl oz water
250g/9oz golden granulated
sugar
100g/3½oz unsalted butter,
cubed
160ml/5½fl oz double cream

Preheat the oven to 180°C/170°C fan/gas 4.

Scatter the cobnuts and sage over a baking sheet and sprinkle with
the salt. Roast for 10-15 minutes, tossing to get an even browning.
Remove and leave to cool.

Turn the oven down to 100°C/90°C fan/gas ¼ and sterilise your
jars and lids (see page 9).

Blitz the cooled toasted nuts in a food processor with a little of the water, adding more if needed, until you have a smooth, thick paste.

In a medium pan, heat the sugar over a medium heat and patiently melt it into a thick amber liquid. Take off the heat and add the butter, whisking for 3-4 minutes to prevent the two from splitting. Put back over a medium heat and, when the butter has melted, very slowly pour in the cream, stirring until combined, and bring to a steady simmer. Stop stirring and boil like this for 1 minute, watching so that it doesn't boil over.

Remove from the heat, stir through the cobnut paste, then pour into hot sterilised jars and seal (see page 15). Once cooled, store in the fridge and eat within 4-6 weeks. Reheat on the hob, with a little extra cream, if you want a looser consistency for drizzling.

Hedgerow Blackberry Cobnut Jam

MAKES 3–4 X 230ML/8FL OZ JARS
LATE SUMMER–AUTUMN | HIGH PECTIN

*Wild blackberries are easy to forage and can been seen in the
later months of the year when you start wrapping up a little more
warmly for your weekend stroll. The bramble bushes, with their
spiky agenda, aren't so appealing to our avian friends – so there are
plenty of berries left for human foragers. Find the berries in hedges,
along river banks, on pathways – almost everywhere. They're easily
recognisable and a good way to start your foraging adventures.*

30g/1oz cobnuts, *husks and
    shells removed and roasted, or
    hazelnuts*
900g/2lb hedgerow
    blackberries, *hulled and rinsed*

30ml/1fl oz water
20ml/¾fl oz lemon juice,
    freshly squeezed
500g/1lb 2oz white sugar

Preheat the oven to 180°C/170°C fan/gas 4.

Roast the cobnuts on a baking sheet for 10–12 minutes until golden
brown. Cool and pat dry with kitchen paper or a clean, dry tea towel.
Turn the oven down to 100°C/90°C fan/gas ¼ and sterilise your jars
and lids (see page 9). Place several small saucers in the freezer.

Place the prepped berries in a jam pan with the water and lemon juice. Soften over a medium heat to create a pulp, stirring so that they don't stick and burn.

Turn up the heat and bring to a rapid boil, then stir in the sugar until completely dissolved. Roughly chop the cobnuts and add to the boiling blackberries, stirring intermittently for 10–12 minutes.

When the bubbles start to get heavier, remove from the heat and start set testing (see page 14) for a hard-set jam. If there isn't an evident wrinkle on the plate, return to the heat and keep testing every minute until there is.

Once at the desired set, skim off any scum and ladle into hot sterilised jars and seal (see page 15). Store unopened in a cool, dark place for up to a year. Once opened, keep in the fridge and eat within 1–2 months.

Wild Plum and Fennel Jam

MAKES 5–6 X 230ML/8FL OZ JARS

LATE SUMMER–AUTUMN | HIGH PECTIN

*Wild plum trees inhabit many gardens and parks throughout the UK.
To distinguish them from their döppelganger, the wild cherry, look at
the flowering buds. If in a cluster and oval, it is a cherry; if singled
out, separated by a twig and round, it is a plum. Wild plums can
range in colour from purple to brown, sometimes green or yellow or
with a reddish tinge, and they vary in size and shape. Use any you can
find for this recipe. Wild fennel can also be found in abundance – use
the bulb, stems and also add some of the leaves to your jam. If you
can't go wild, then opt for the garden or store-bought variety.*

900g/2lb wild plums, *pitted
  weight*
300g/10½oz wild fennel, *bulb
  and stalks*

90ml/3fl oz water
50ml/2fl oz lemon juice, *freshly
  squeezed*
700g/1lb 9oz white sugar

82

Sterilise your jars and lids (see page 9) and place several small saucers in the freezer.

Cut the pitted plums into 2–3cm/¾–1¼in cubes and chop the fennel into 2cm/¾in chunks. Place both in a jam pan with the water and lemon juice. Soften over a medium-high heat until it becomes pulp, stirring often so that it doesn't stick and burn.

Turn up the heat and bring to a rapid boil, then stir through the sugar until completely dissolved. Bring the jam back to the boil, stirring intermittently for 8–12 minutes and watching that it doesn't stick and burn.

When the bubbles start to get heavier, remove from the heat and start set testing (see page 14) for a hard-set jam. If there isn't an evident wrinkle on the plate, return to the heat and keep testing every minute until there is.

Once at the desired set, skim off any scum and ladle the hot jam into hot sterilised jars and seal (see page 15). Store unopened in a cool, dark place for up to a year. Once opened, keep in the fridge and eat within 1–2 months.

Damson and Lavender Cheese

MAKES 8-12 MOULDS | LATE SUMMER-AUTUMN | HIGH PECTIN

*A hedgerow is one of my favourite places to forage; it provides the
perfect opportunity to venture into nature and gather its offerings.
Damsons are one of these gifts. Although generally too tart to be eaten
alone, they are great when sweetened into individual fruit cheeses.
Damsons are found almost everywhere in the UK from late August into
September. Add the lavender from your own garden, or ask for some
from a friendly neighbour. These little cheeses will keep long enough to
give as Christmas presents – nature's gift that keeps on giving.*

1-1.25kg/2lb 4oz-2lb 12oz
damsons, *rinsed and twigs
removed*
2-3 tsp dried lavender flowers
650-750ml/1-1⅓ pints water
40ml/1¼fl oz lemon juice,
freshly squeezed, strained

8-12 lavender heads with
stalks, *rinsed and dried*
400-600g/14oz-1lb 5oz
white sugar
Light olive oil, *for greasing*

Place the damsons in a large pan with the dried lavender and just
cover with the water. Bring to a rapid boil, then turn down the
heat and simmer for 50 minutes-1 hour, stirring and mashing
intermittently.

Push the pulp through a fine-mesh sieve into a bowl in batches,
discarding the damson stones and skins. Weigh the pulp and place in

a large jam pan over a medium-low heat with the lemon juice, and warm through. Measure out 200g/7oz of sugar for every 250g/9oz of pulp and stir until completely dissolved.

Bring to a 'ploppy' boil over a medium heat for 35-40 minutes, stirring to control the heavy bubbles until it thickens into a paste. This gets messy and I often cover the pan with a splatter guard to protect the walls and ceilings.

Preheat the oven to the lowest setting possible and lightly grease 80ml/2½fl oz muffin trays or similar sized moulds. Place 1–2 lavender heads into the bottom of each mould, spoon over 1–2 teaspoons of paste to set them in place, then fill the moulds until they are 5ml/1 tsp from the top. Bang the tray on a surface to level the mixture, then level out the surface of each using a spatula. Cook in the oven for 30–35 minutes.

When ready, flip out the cheeses from the moulds and keep in Tupperware in the fridge between layers of non-stick baking paper until you are ready to individually wrap, with baking paper and string, and label for gifting. They will keep in the fridge for up to 6–8 months.

Crab Apple and Chilli Jelly

MAKES 5–6 X 230ML/8FL OZ JARS

LATE SUMMER–AUTUMN | HIGH PECTIN

Crab apples, although incredibly sharp in taste, are delicious when you 'just add sugar'. As they're extremely common in England, Wales and southern Scotland, you can spot them around the countryside and in the city. High in pectin, they make a great base for other fruits that don't contain as much pectin, so you can get achievable sets in your jams or jellies. Or you can just add herbs, spices or flowers and create a jelly float, as in this recipe with a little kick of chilli.

1.4kg/3lb 3oz crab apples, scrubbed and roughly chopped (with skins, pips and cores)

5 strips of pared lemon peel, unwaxed

1.7 litres/3 pints water

650–750g/1lb 7oz–1lb 10oz white sugar

1 tsp chilli flakes

30ml/1fl oz lemon juice, *freshly squeezed, strained*

Place the prepped apples and lemon peel in a large pot or pan and completely cover with the water. Bring to a simmer over a medium heat for about 35 minutes, gently crushing the apples without over-mashing.

Strain through a large square of muslin, tied up by all corners and suspended over a bowl, or use a jelly bag. Leave for up to 8 hours or overnight, without being tempted to squeeze the bag.

The next day, sterilise your jars and lids (see page 9) and place several small saucers in the freezer. Measure out the apple liquid; for every 200ml/7fl oz of liquid, weigh out 140g/5oz of sugar. Mix the chilli flakes through the sugar. Pour the apple liquid into a jam pan with the lemon juice and bring to a rapid boil over the highest heat, then stir through the sugar until completely dissolved.

When the jelly reaches 104°C/219°F on a sugar thermometer, or when it's been at a vigorous boil for at least 5-6 minutes, remove from the heat and start set testing (see page 14) for a hard-set jam. If there isn't an evident wrinkle on the plate, return to the heat and keep testing every minute until there is.

Once at the desired set, skim off any scum and immediately ladle or pour the hot jelly into hot sterilised jars and seal (see page 15). Store unopened in a cool, dark place for up to a year. Once opened, keep in the fridge and eat within 3-4 months.

Hawthorn and Wild Fennel Seed Jelly

MAKES 4–5 X 230ML/8FL OZ JARS
LATE SUMMER–AUTUMN | HIGH PECTIN

*The hawthorn is Britain's most common hedgerow tree, so super easy
and accessible to forage to make an abundance of jelly preserves
in early autumn. Hawthorn berries are also thought to have heart
health benefits as they contain antioxidants. To harvest your wild or
homegrown fennel seeds (you can use store-bought too), let the fennel
heads go to seed. Simply snip off the heads into a paper bag when
they have started to brown, and leave to dry like this for 1–2 weeks.
Crumble them into a bowl with your hands and shake the bowl,
removing any stems as they work their way to the top. Scoop out any
finer powdered fennel residue, and then the seeds are ready to use.*

1.6kg/3lb 8oz hawthorn
  berries, *rinsed and plucked
  from stalks/leaves*
1.8 litres/3¼ pints water
4 strips of pared lemon peel,
  unwaxed

50ml/2fl oz lemon juice, *freshly
  squeezed, strained*
750–800g/1lb 10oz–1lb 12oz
  white sugar
1¼ tsp fennel seeds

Place the prepped berries in a large pot or pan with the water and
lemon peel and bring to a simmer over a medium heat. After about
30 minutes, gently crush the berries without over-mashing them.

Strain through a large square of muslin tied up by all corners and suspended over a bowl, or use a jelly bag. Leave for up to 8 hours (or overnight), without being tempted to squeeze the bag.

The next day, sterilise your jars and lids (see page 9) and place several small saucers in the freezer.

Measure out the hawthorn liquid; for every 200ml/7fl oz of liquid, weigh out 160g/5¾oz of sugar. Pour the hawthorn liquid into a jam pan with the lemon juice and bring to a rapid boil over the highest heat, then stir through the sugar until completely dissolved.

When the jelly reaches 104°C/219°F on a sugar thermometer, or when it's been at a vigorous boil for at least 5–6 minutes, remove from the heat and start set testing (see page 14) for a hard-set jam. If there isn't an evident wrinkle on the plate, return to the heat and keep testing every minute until there is.

Once at the desired set, carefully skim off any scum, stir through the fennel seeds and quickly ladle into hot sterilised jars and seal (see page 15). Store unopened in a cool, dark place for up to a year. Once opened, keep in the fridge and eat within 3–4 months.

Rosehip and Nasturtium Jelly

MAKES 5–6 X 230ML/8FL OZ JARS

LATE SUMMER–AUTUMN | HIGH PECTIN

Both rosehips and nasturtiums are extremely high in vitamin C, so they make great tinctures when you're feeling a bit under the weather come winter. Just put a teaspoon of this jelly into boiling water for a 'rosehip toddy' to tackle any sore throats, coughs or colds.

1kg/2lb 4oz rosehips, *rinsed and plucked from stalks/leaves, roughly chopped*

500g/1lb 2oz Bramley or crab apples, *scrubbed and roughly chopped (with skins, pips and cores)*

2.2 litres/4 pints water

4 strips of pared lemon peel

20 nasturtium leaves and/or flowers, *3–4 leaves reserved and finely chopped*

40ml/1¼fl oz lemon juice, *freshly squeezed, strained*

700–750g/1lb 9oz–1lb 10oz white sugar

Place the prepped rosehips and apples in a large pot with the water and lemon peel and bring to a simmer over a medium heat. After 30 minutes, gently crush the hips and apples without over-mashing.

Remove from the heat, add the nasturtium leaves and/or flowers and steep while cooling for about 20 minutes. Strain through a large square of muslin tied up by all corners and suspended over a bowl, or use a jelly bag. Leave for up to 8 hours (or overnight), without being tempted to squeeze the bag.

The next day, sterilise your jars and lids (see page 9) and place several small saucers in the freezer. Measure the rosehip/apple liquid; for every 200ml/7fl oz of liquid, weigh out 160g/5¾oz sugar. Pour the rosehip liquid into a jam pan with the lemon juice and bring to a rapid boil over the highest heat, then stir through the sugar until completely dissolved.

When the jelly reaches 104°C/219°F on a sugar thermometer, or when it's been at a vigorous boil for at least 6–8 minutes, remove from the heat and start set testing (see page 14) for a hard-set jam. If there isn't an evident wrinkle on the plate, return to the heat and keep testing every minute until there is.

Once at the desired set, carefully skim off any scum and stir through the chopped nasturtium leaves and ladle into hot sterilised jars and seal (see page 15). Store unopened in a cool, dark place for up to a year. Once opened, keep in the fridge and eat within 3–4 months.

Sloe (Blackthorn) and Gin Jelly

MAKES 4–5 X 230ML/8FL OZ JARS | AUTUMN | HIGH PECTIN

*I've made sloe gin for years and years, but this recipe was the
perfect opportunity to turn that concept into a jelly preserve.
Sloes seem to be the most popular hedgerow berry that people
forage and go back for every year. Pick them between September
and October and change your harvesting spot each year;
you might also stumble across a juniper bush too, which will
help you to create that distinctive gin taste in this jelly.*

1kg/2lb 4oz sloes, *rinsed and
plucked from stalks/leaves*
500g/1lb 2oz Bramley or crab
apples, *unwaxed or washed
and scrubbed, roughly chopped
(with skins, pips and cores)*
1.5 litres/2¾ pints water

4 strips of pared lemon peel,
unwaxed
8 juniper berries
30ml/1fl oz lemon juice, *freshly
squeezed, strained*
700–750g/1lb 9oz–1lb 10oz
white sugar
50ml/2fl oz gin

Place the prepped sloes and apples in a large pot or pan with the
water, lemon peel and juniper berries and bring to a simmer over a
medium heat. After about 30 minutes, gently crush the fruit without
over-mashing.

Strain through a large square of muslin tied up by all corners and suspended over a bowl, or a jelly bag. Leave for up to 8 hours or overnight, without being tempted to squeeze the bag.

The next day, sterilise your jars and lids (see page 9) and place several small saucers in the freezer. Measure the sloe/apple liquid; for every 200ml/7fl oz of liquid, weigh out 160g/5¾oz of sugar. Pour the liquid into a jam pan with the lemon juice and bring to a rapid boil over the highest heat, then stir through the sugar until completely dissolved. Bring back to a rapid boil and add the gin.

When the jelly reaches 104°C/219°F on a sugar thermometer, or when it's been at a vigorous boil for at least 6–8 minutes, remove from the heat and start set testing (see page 14) for a hard-set jam. If there isn't an evident wrinkle on the plate, return to the heat and keep testing every minute until there is.

Once at the desired set, carefully skim off any scum and quickly ladle the hot liquid jelly into hot sterilised jars and seal (see page 15). Store unopened in a cool, dark place for up to a year. Once opened, keep in the fridge and eat within 3–4 months.

Quince and Lemon Thyme
Paste or Cheese

MAKES 5–6 X 230ML/8FL OZ JARS/12–20 X SQUARES/6–8 MOULDS

WINTER | HIGH PECTIN

Quince is a perfect preserving fruit as it is high in pectin and, if cooked long enough with enough lemon juice, turns the prettiest pink hue. Make this recipe using the discarded pulp from the quince jelly on page 122.

1–1.25kg/2lb 4oz–2lb 12oz
  quince pulp (see page 122)
640–800g/1lb 7oz–1lb 12oz
  white sugar
250–300ml/9–10fl oz water

100ml/3½fl oz lemon juice,
  freshly squeezed, strained
4 sprigs of lemon thyme
Light olive oil, *for greasing*
  (optional)

Preheat the oven to 100°C/90°C fan/gas ¼ and, if making quince paste, sterilise your jars and lids (see page 9). If making the harder-set quince cheese, line a 20 x 30cm/8 x 12in-deep baking tin with non-stick baking paper, or lightly oil the holes in smaller 80ml/2½fl oz muffin trays or similar sized moulds.

Weigh the quince pulp; for every 250g/9oz of pulp, weigh out 160g/5¾oz of sugar. Transfer the sugar onto a large baking sheet lined with non-stick baking paper and warm in the oven for 5 minutes.

Place the quince pulp in a food processor with the water and blend until smooth and thick – this may need to be done in batches. Put into a jam pan with the lemon juice and lemon thyme sprigs and start to warm through, stirring intermittently.

Once warmed through, add the warmed sugar, stirring until completely dissolved. Bring to a 'ploppy' boil over a medium-low heat and cook for 45 minutes–1 hour, stirring only to control the heavy bubbles. This gets messy and covering it with a splatter guard can help to protect the walls and ceilings.

Once it has pinkened in hue, remove the thyme stalks and if making paste, carefully pour into hot sterilised jars and seal (see page 15). If making quince cheese, fill your baking tin or moulds and cook in the oven for 30–35 minutes.

Keep the paste in sealed jars for up to a year and once opened, refrigerate for 6–8 months. For the cheese, flip out the contents from the tray and cut into desired shapes or empty the moulds and keep in Tupperware in the fridge between layers of non-stick baking paper for up to 8 months.

Medlar and Garden Rosemary Jelly

MAKES 5–6 X 230ML/8FL OZ JARS | WINTER | LOW PECTIN

I've been making my medlar jelly for years and I've been dying to share this recipe. I couldn't think of a more perfect place than in this National Trust book. You need to fully ripen medlars to make a successful jelly – what we call 'to blet'. That means they become low in pectin, so to get the required pectin into your set you can either add just-ripe apples or a few harder medlars. I tend to add apples, as you'll discover below.

1kg/2lb 4oz medlars, *bletted in a warm place for 2–3 weeks, soft to touch, rinsed and quartered*

300g/10½oz Bramley or crab apples, *unwaxed or washed and scrubbed, roughly chopped (with skins, pips and cores)*

1.5 litres/2¾ pints water

4–6 sprigs of rosemary

4 strips of pared lemon peel, *unwaxed*

750–800g/1lb 10oz–1lb 12oz white sugar

50ml/2fl oz lemon juice, *freshly squeezed, strained*

Place the prepped medlars and apples in a large pot or pan with the water, most of the rosemary and the lemon peel, and bring to a simmer over a medium heat. After about 30 minutes, gently crush the fruit without over-mashing.

Strain through a large square of muslin tied up by all corners and suspended over a bowl, or use a jelly bag. Leave for up to 8 hours or overnight, without being tempted to squeeze the bag.

The next day, sterilise your jars and lids (see page 9) and place several small saucers in the freezer. Measure the medlar/apple liquid; for every 200ml/7fl oz of liquid, weigh out 160g/5¾oz of sugar. Pour the liquid into a jam pan with the lemon juice and bring to a rapid boil over the highest heat, then stir through the sugar until completely dissolved.

When the jelly reaches 104°C/219°F on a sugar thermometer, or when it's been at a vigorous boil for at least 4–6 minutes, remove from the heat and start set testing (see page 14) for a hard set jam. If there isn't an evident wrinkle on the plate, return to the heat and keep testing every minute until there is.

Once at the desired set, set up your hot sterilised jars with a small cutting of the remaining rosemary in each, skim off any scum on the jelly and quickly ladle it into the jars and seal (see page 15). Store unopened in a cool, dark place for up to a year. Once opened, keep in the fridge and eat within 3–4 months.

Chapter 3

Jelly Floats

To add a more sophisticated look to your jellies, I've created this jelly float chapter. Jellies are preserves where the juice is extracted from the pulp of fruits and cooked with sugar to create a crystal-clear, glass-like preserve, much like a stained glass piece in a chapel window.

These jellies should not be confused with jelly desserts, which are fruit-flavoured sugar crystals containing gelatine dissolved in boiling water, set and cooled in the fridge and eaten within a week. The preserving jellies in this chapter are made without gelatine; instead, they rely on pectin, the gelling substance present in all fruits. They are generally smoother and softer in texture, without the rubbery feel of jelly/jello, and can be kept in their sealed jars unopened for up to a year.

My twist is to add floating fruits, spices, herbs and flowers into these crystal-clear displays, as if the jar is the frame, capturing nature in motion as the elements are suspended while the jelly slowly cools and sets. I've been wanting to write a recipe for a wine-poached pear in a vanilla jelly for a long time now, and this book is the perfect opportunity for me to share this kind of 'outside the box' idea.

Jelly preserves were traditionally eaten at the end of magnificent feasts, with marmalades, jams and cheese, and were restricted to royalty and the very wealthy, as sugar was very expensive in the sixteenth and seventeenth centuries. It wasn't until the Industrial Revolution in the nineteenth century that sugar was readily affordable for the common people, and fruit preservation before this time often involved enclosing fruits in honey.

Honey was a traditional means to preserve things due to its antibacterial properties; it has no moisture, and bacteria need moisture to live and replicate. Honey, however, doesn't extract enough water from fruit, so the pectin isn't as effective. This isn't ideal when it comes to making jelly, where you require a firm gelled set, so sugar is essential.

To achieve a good set on a preserve jelly, it's best to use fruits high in pectin, such as quince, currants, apples and lemons. If your fruits aren't high in pectin, you will need a helping hand, and that's when commercial powdered pectins or sugars with added pectin (such as jam sugar) can come to your aid.

There's a slightly more involved and time-consuming method of making jelly where you juice or cook and soften prepared fruit, usually with all its skin and glory, with a quantity of water, then pass it through a jelly bag or a square of muslin/cheesecloth, to allow it to drip into a bowl overnight (8–12 hours). Do not be tempted to squeeze the bag as this often clouds the crystal-clear effect. The fruit liquid is collected, measured and then heated before sugar is dissolved into it. Bring it to a temperature of at least 104°C/219°F, then wrinkle/set test it (see page 14) for a firm set, before pouring it into sterilised jars to cool.

Setting tends to happen quickly with jellies, so there's an art to suspending fruit, flowers, herbs and spices and it can take a few goes to master the process. But practice makes perfect, and you will get the hang of it when you get used to the speed you have to work at and start to see the signals that your jelly is beginning to set. If you overcook the jelly, you will see it start to set too quickly while you're jarring, meaning that there is not enough fluidity in the jelly for your ingredients to slowly set in motion. Yet you also don't want to undercook it, as the bits will float directly to the top or sink to the bottom and the jelly won't have the correct density to look as if the contents are suspended in space.

Gauging this is key, so have several saucers in the freezer ready for set testing. For a firm set you want your wrinkle (when pushed) to be like the skin wrinkle atop of heated milk: clear, concise and evident. Keep testing until you find that happy medium.

When at that turning point, rest the jelly for 3–4 minutes and very quickly ladle into hot sterilised jars 1–2mm from the top rim. Seal and turn upside down. If you reach the correct gelling point, your jelly will start to congeal and then, as if by magic, the added ingredients will suspend midway through setting when the jar is turned the right way up.

Elderflower Float Jelly

MAKES 5–6 X 230ML/8FL OZ JARS | EARLY SUMMER | LOW PECTIN

*There's nothing prettier than elderflowers gently floating across
a jar, set in jelly. It does take some patience and vigilance to
achieve this, as you can miss the moment when the jelly starts to gel.
Keep turning the jars until you get it right – practice makes perfect.*

100g/3½fl oz (20–24)
    elderflower heads
1.1 litres/1¾ pints water
1 lemon, *unwaxed*

1kg/2lb 4oz jam sugar
30ml/1fl oz lemon juice, *freshly
    squeezed, strained*

Place the elderflowers, reserving 5–6 smaller heads, in a large bowl with the water, the juice of 1 lemon and the squeezed-out lemon halves. Rest a plate on top so that all the ingredients are submerged in the water and place in the fridge for at least 24 hours.

The next day, sterilise your jars and lids (see page 9) and place several small saucers in the freezer. Strain the elderflower liquid through muslin draped over a fine mesh sieve, and measure into a jam pan. For every 200ml/7fl oz of liquid, weigh out 200g/7oz of jam sugar. Add the lemon juice to the pan and bring to a rapid boil over the highest heat, then stir through the sugar until completely dissolved.

When the jelly reaches 104°C/219°F on a sugar thermometer, or when it's been at a vigorous boil for at least 8–10 minutes, remove from the heat and start set testing (see page 101) for a hard-set jam. If there isn't an evident wrinkle on the plate, return to the heat and keep testing every minute until there is.

Once at the desired set, let it stand for 3–4 minutes and carefully skim off any scum while you set up your sterilised jars with an elderflower sprig in each. Quickly ladle in the hot jelly and seal (see page 15). Turn the sealed jars upside down and allow to set slightly for 30–40 minutes, so that the flower slowly floats upwards in the setting jelly.

Store upright in a cool, dark place for up to a year. Once opened, keep in the fridge and eat within 3–4 months.

Strawberry Suspension in Elderflower Jelly

MAKES 5–6 X 230ML/8FL OZ JARS | SUMMER | LOW PECTIN

With the addition of strawberries in this elderflower jelly, the timings of your set will differ. Watch it carefully, testing every now and again to see if it's gelling before turning the jars upside down to watch the strawberries slowly set in motion. Try tiny wild strawberries if you have a small yield; they are perfect as they're lighter in weight.

100g/3½oz (20–24) elderflower heads

1.1 litres/1¾ pints water

1 lemon, *unwaxed*

1–1.2kg/2lb 4oz–2lb 11oz jam sugar

30ml/1fl oz lemon juice, *freshly squeezed, strained*

90–100g/3¼–3½oz strawberries, *chopped into 1cm/½in pieces*

Place the elderflowers in a large bowl with the water, the juice of 1 lemon and the squeezed-out lemon halves. Rest a plate on top so that all the ingredients are submerged in the water and place in the fridge for at least 24 hours.

The next day, sterilise your jars and lids (see page 9) and place several small saucers in the freezer. Strain the elderflower liquid through muslin draped over a fine mesh sieve, and measure into a jam pan. For every 200ml/7fl oz of liquid, weigh out 210g/7½oz of jam sugar. Add the lemon juice to the pan and bring to a rapid boil over the highest heat, then stir through the sugar until completely dissolved.

When the jelly reaches 104°C/219°F on a sugar thermometer, or when it's been at a vigorous boil for at least 10–12 minutes, remove from the heat and start set testing (see page 101) for a hard-set jam. If there isn't an evident wrinkle on the plate, return to the heat and keep testing every minute until there is.

Once at the desired set, let it stand for 3–4 minutes and carefully skim off any scum while you set up your sterilised jars with a few strawberry pieces in each. Quickly ladle in the hot jelly and seal (see page 15). Turn the sealed jars upside down and allow to set slightly for 1 hour–1 hour 20 minutes so that the fruit slowly floats upwards in the setting jelly.

Store upright in a cool, dark place for up to a year. Once opened, keep in the fridge and eat within 3–4 months.

Whitecurrant and Blueberry Bubble Jelly

MAKES 4–5 X 230ML/8FL OZ JARS | SUMMER | HIGH PECTIN

These jelly preserves are meant to be decadent and for decadent occasions: a treat, gifted for their beauty. Suspended blueberries here mimic black bubbles floating up like the bubbles of your favourite sparkling wine, the whitecurrant jelly providing the perfect backdrop for this illusion.

900g/2lb whitecurrants, *rinsed and plucked from stalks*

550ml/18½fl oz water

3 strips of pared lemon peel, *unwaxed*

400–500g/14oz–1lb 2oz white sugar

30ml/1fl oz lemon juice, *freshly squeezed and strained*

100ml/3½fl oz sparkling wine, cava or prosecco

200g/7oz blueberries

Place the prepared currants in a large pot or pan with the water and lemon peel. Bring to a simmer over a medium heat and after 15–20 minutes, gently crush the currants without over-mashing.

Strain through a large square of muslin tied up by all corners and suspended over a bowl, or use a jelly bag. Leave for up to 8 hours or overnight, without being tempted to squeeze the bag.

The next day, sterilise your jars and lids (see page 9) and place several small saucers in the freezer.

Measure out the whitecurrant liquid; for every 200ml/7fl oz of liquid, weigh out 140g/5oz of sugar. Pour the liquid into a jam pan with the lemon juice and bring to a rapid boil over the highest heat, then stir through the sugar until completely dissolved.

When the jelly reaches 104°C/219°F on a sugar thermometer, or when it's been at a vigorous boil for at least 6–8 minutes, remove from the heat and start set testing (see page 101) for a hard-set jam. If there isn't an evident wrinkle on the plate, return to the heat and keep testing every minute until there is.

Once at the desired set, stir through the sparkling wine and set your jars up with 50g/1¾oz of blueberries in each. Quickly ladle over the hot jelly and seal (see page 15). Turn the sealed jars upside down and allow to set slightly for about 5–8 minutes so the blueberries slowly float upwards.

Store upright in a cool, dark place for up to a year. Once opened, keep in the fridge and eat within 3–4 months.

Raspberry Cacao Nib Jam

MAKES 3–4 X 230ML/8FL OZ JARS | SUMMER | LOW PECTIN

Lots of people love raspberry jam, but some love it more without the seeds. As a twist on this, why not try to extract the seeds and add cacao nibs instead – like a raspberry and chocolate chip version.

1kg/2lb 4oz raspberries,
  gently rinsed
150ml/5fl oz water

40ml/1¼fl oz lemon juice,
  freshly squeezed
500g/1lb 2oz white sugar
1½ tbsp cacao nibs

Sterilise your jars and lids (see page 9) and place several small saucers in the freezer.

Add the berries to a large pot or pan with the water. Bring to a simmer over a medium heat and after 10–12 minutes, gently crush the berries with a wooden spoon to create a pulp.

Remove from the heat and push through a fine-mesh sieve, extracting the seeds and discarding. Place berries into a jam pan with the lemon juice and bring to a rapid boil over a high heat. Stir through the sugar until completely dissolved and bring back to a rapid boil.

When the jelly reaches 104°C/219°F on a sugar thermometer, or when it's been at a vigorous boil for at least 6–8 minutes, remove from the heat and start set testing (see page 14) for a hard-set jam. If there isn't an evident wrinkle on the plate, return to the heat and keep testing every minute until there is.

Once at the desired set, skim off any scum, stir through the cacao nibs and quickly ladle into hot sterilised jars and seal (see page 15). Store unopened in a cool, dark place for up to a year. Once opened, keep in the fridge and eat within 1–2 months.

Blackberries in an Apple Tree

MAKES 5–6 X 230ML/8FL OZ JARS

AUTUMN | APPLES HIGH IN PECTIN

*I like to really pack the jars with blackberries for this one –
less floating action, but glimmers of clear jelly amongst the
darker tones of the blackberries create a dramatic effect.*

1kg/2lb 4oz Bramley apples, *unwaxed or scrubbed and roughly chopped (with skins, pips and cores)*
3 strips of pared lemon peel, *unwaxed*

1.2 litres/2 pints water
650–750g/1lb 7oz–1lb 10oz white sugar
30ml/1fl oz lemon juice, *freshly squeezed, strained*
350–400g/12–14oz blackberries

Place the prepared apples and lemon peel in a large pot or pan with the water. Bring to a simmer over a medium heat and after 25–30 minutes, gently crush the softened apple with a wooden spoon, without over-mashing.

Strain through a large square of muslin tied up by all corners and suspended over a bowl, or use a jelly bag. Leave for up to 8 hours or overnight, without being tempted to squeeze the bag.

The next day, sterilise your jars and lids (see page 9) and place several small saucers in the freezer.

Measure out the apple liquid; for every 200ml/7fl oz of liquid, weigh out 140g/5oz of sugar. Pour the apple liquid into a jam pan with the lemon juice and bring to a rapid boil over the highest heat. Pour in the measure of sugar and stir through until completely dissolved.

When the jelly reaches 104°C/219°F on a sugar thermometer, or when it's been at a vigorous boil for 5–6 minutes, remove from the heat and start set testing (see page 101) for a hard-set jam. If there isn't an evident wrinkle on the plate, return to the heat and keep testing every minute until there is.

Once at the desired set, rest for 3–4 minutes off the heat and set your jars up with 4–5 tightly packed blackberries in each. Skim off any scum and quickly ladle into hot sterilised jars and seal (see page 15). Turn upside down and allow to set slightly for 4–6 minutes before turning so the berries slowly float upwards.

Store upright in a cool, dark place for up to a year. Once opened, keep in the fridge and eat within 3–4 months.

Raspberries Floating in Vanilla Jelly

MAKES 4–5 X 230ML/8FL OZ JARS

SUMMER | APPLES HIGH IN PECTIN

Using a vanilla jelly base as a float makes the prettiest raspberry-speckled jelly. The raspberries float upwards, as if to escape the jar.

1.4kg/3lb 3oz Bramley apples, *unwaxed or scrubbed and roughly chopped (with skins, pips and cores)*
5 strips of pared lemon peel, *unwaxed*
1.7 litres/3 pints water

650–750g/1lb 7oz–1lb 10oz white sugar
30ml/1fl oz lemon juice, *freshly squeezed, strained*
½ vanilla pod, *split, seeds scraped*
160–200g/5¾–7oz raspberries

Place the prepared apples and lemon peel in a large pot or pan with the water. Bring to a simmer over a medium heat and after 25–30 minutes, gently crush the softened apple with a wooden spoon, without over-mashing.

Strain through a large square of muslin tied up by all corners and suspended over a bowl, or use a jelly bag. Leave for up to 8 hours or overnight, without being tempted to squeeze the bag.

The next day, sterilise your jars and lids (see page 9) and place several small saucers in the freezer. Measure out the apple liquid; for every 200ml/7fl oz of liquid, weigh out 140g/5oz of sugar. Pour the apple

liquid into a jam pan with the lemon juice and bring to a rapid boil over the highest heat. Mix the vanilla seeds and pod through the sugar, then pour into the pan, stirring until completely dissolved.

When the jelly reaches 104°C/219°F on a sugar thermometer, or when it's been at a vigorous boil for 5–6 minutes, remove from the heat and start set testing (see page 101) for a hard-set jam. If there isn't an evident wrinkle on the plate, return to the heat and keep testing every minute until there is.

Once at the desired set, rest for 3–4 minutes off the heat and set your jars up with 4–5 raspberries in each. Pick out the vanilla pod (if using) from the pan, skim off any scum and quickly ladle into hot sterilised jars and seal (see page 15). Turn upside down and allow to set slightly for 4–6 minutes so the berries slowly float upwards.

Store upright in a cool, dark place for up to a year. Once opened, keep in the fridge and eat within 3–4 months.

Herbed Crab Apple Jelly

MAKES 4–5 X 230ML/8FL OZ JARS

LATE SUMMER | CRAB APPLES HIGH IN PECTIN

Herbs look ever so pretty suspended in jelly preserves. Chop, tear, slice or leave them whole. Some recipes call for macerating the herbs in a fruit-sugar mix; however, when it comes to the softer, more delicate varieties, like basil or mint, you want to add them at the end, so that flecks of their flavour bounce intermittently on your palate.

1.4kg/2lb 4oz crab apples, *washed and roughly chopped (with skins, pips and cores)*

5 strips of pared lemon peel, *unwaxed*

1.7 litres/3 pints water

650–750g/1lb 7oz–1lb 10oz white sugar

30ml/1fl oz lemon juice, *freshly squeezed, strained*

6–8 basil or mint leaves, *finely chopped*

Place the prepared apples and lemon peel in a large pot or pan with the water. Bring to a simmer over a medium heat and after 20 minutes, gently crush the softened apple with a wooden spoon, without over-mashing.

Strain through a large square of muslin tied up by all corners and suspended over a bowl, or use a jelly bag. Leave for up to 8 hours or overnight, without being tempted to squeeze the bag.

The next day, sterilise your jars and lids (see page 9) and place several small saucers in the freezer.

Measure out the apple liquid; for every 200ml/7fl oz of liquid weigh out 140g/5oz of sugar. Pour the apple liquid into a jam pan with the lemon juice and bring to a rapid boil over the highest heat, then stir through the sugar until completely dissolved.

When the jelly reaches 104°C/219°F on a sugar thermometer, or when it's been at a vigorous boil for 5-6 minutes, remove from the heat and start set testing (see page 101) for a hard-set jam. If there isn't an evident wrinkle on the plate, return to the heat and keep testing every minute until there is.

Once at the desired set, let it stand for 2-3 minutes. Skim off any scum and stir through the chopped mint or basil and quickly ladle into hot sterilised jars and seal (see page 15). Store unopened in a cool, dark place for up to a year. Once opened, keep in the fridge and eat within 3-4 months.

Mini Poached Pears in Jelly

MAKES 5–6 X 230ML/8FL OZ JARS

AUTUMN–WINTER | APPLES HIGH IN PECTIN

I've been wanting to develop this recipe for years, ever since I discovered miniature pears. If you can't find mini pears in your local shop or supermarket, just poach pear pieces instead.

1kg/2lb 4oz Bramley apples, *unwaxed or scrubbed and roughly chopped (with skins, pips and cores)*

3 strips of pared lemon peel, *unwaxed*

1.2 litres/2 pints water

5–6 firm miniature pears, *peeled*

½ vanilla pod, *split, seeds scraped*

550–650g/1lb 4oz–1lb 7oz white sugar

30ml/1fl oz lemon juice, *freshly squeezed, strained*

For the poaching liquor:

200ml/7fl oz white wine

100ml/3½fl oz water

70g/2½oz white sugar

3 slices of ginger

3 strips of pared orange peel, *unwaxed*

1 orange, *juice*

1 tsp juniper berries

4 cloves

1 small cinnamon stick

Place the prepared apples and lemon peel in a large pot or pan with the water. Bring to a simmer over a medium heat and after 20 minutes, gently crush the softened apple with a wooden spoon, without over-mashing.

Strain through a large square of muslin tied up by all corners and suspended over a bowl, or use a jelly bag. Leave for up to 8 hours or overnight, without being tempted to squeeze the bag.

Warm all the ingredients for the poaching liquor in a pan to dissolve the sugar, then bring to a simmer, add the pears and poach for 5 minutes. Place in a Tupperware container to cool. Once cooled, refrigerate for up to 8 hours or overnight.

The next day, sterilise your jars and lids (see page 9) and place several small saucers in the freezer. Measure out the apple liquid; for every 200ml/7fl oz of liquid, weigh out 150g/5½oz of sugar. Mix the vanilla seeds and pod through the sugar. Pour the apple liquid into a jam pan with the lemon juice and bring to a rapid boil over the highest heat, then stir through the sugar until completely dissolved.

When the jelly reaches 104°C/219°F on a sugar thermometer, or when it's been at a vigorous boil for 5–6 minutes, remove from the heat and start set testing (see page 101) for a hard set. If there isn't an evident wrinkle on the plate, return to the heat and keep testing every minute until there is.

Once at the desired set, set up your sterilised jars with one mini pear in each. Ladle over the hot jelly and seal (see page 15). Store unopened in a cool, dark place for up to 8–10 months. Once opened, keep in the fridge and eat within 3–4 weeks.

Pepper Storm Lemon Jelly

MAKES 4–5 X 230ML/8FL OZ JARS

AUTUMN–WINTER | LEMONS HIGH IN PECTIN

Use this jelly to macerate pineapple chunks before roasting them, and serve as a quick dessert with a scoop of coconut ice-cream melted on top. You can also use the jelly to soothe a winter cold's sore throat by dissolving a teaspoon into a warming toddy.

1.1kg/2lb 7oz juicy lemons, *unwaxed or scrubbed*
800ml/1⅓ pints boiling water

900g–1kg/2lb–2lb 4oz jam sugar
1½ tsp freshly ground black pepper

Juice the lemons into a large bowl; roughly chop the remaining skin, pith, pips and all, and add to the juice. Pour over the boiling water, cover and steep for up to 6–8 hours or overnight.

The next day, sterilise your jars and lids (see page 9) and place several small saucers in the freezer. Strain the lemon liquid through muslin draped over a fine-mesh sieve and measure into a jam pan. Bring to the boil over a high heat.

For every 200ml/7fl oz of liquid, weigh out 180g/6oz of sugar, add to the pan and stir through until completely dissolved. Bring back to a rapid boil and when the jelly reaches 104°C/219°F on a sugar thermometer, or when it's been at a vigorous boil for 10–15 minutes, remove from the heat and start set testing (see page 101) for a hard-set jam. If there isn't an evident wrinkle on the plate, return to the heat and keep testing every minute until there is.

Once at the desired set, let it stand for 3–4 minutes, skim off any scum and stir through the pepper. Quickly ladle into hot sterilised jars and seal (see page 15). The pepper should evenly disperse through the jars as the jelly sets.

Store unopened in a cool, dark place for up to a year. Once opened, keep in the fridge and eat within 3–4 months.

Chamomile Amongst Lime Orchard

MAKES 3–4 X 230ML/8FL OZ JARS

AUTUMN–WINTER | LIMES HIGH IN PECTIN

*I love adding chamomile to my preserves – especially with sharper
fruits. Chamomile tends to mellow out their tartness with its calming
properties, leaving you feeling as if you are skipping through
flowered fruit orchards on a hot summer's day – well, me anyway.*

1.1kg/2lb 7oz juicy limes,
   unwaxed or scrubbed
5 strips of pared lemon peel,
   unwaxed
800ml/1⅓ pints boiling water

600–700g/1lb 5oz–1lb 9oz jam
   sugar
1 tbsp dried chamomile or
   loose chamomile tea

Sterilise your jars and lids (see page 9) and place several small saucers in the freezer.

Juice the limes into a large pan and roughly chop the remaining skin, pith, pips and all, and add to the juice with the lemon peel. Pour over the boiling water, bring to the boil and simmer for 10 minutes.

Strain through muslin draped over a fine-mesh sieve and measure into a jam pan. Bring to the boil over a high heat. For every 200ml/7fl oz of juice, weigh out 180g/6oz of sugar and mix through the chamomile. Pour the sugar into the boiling lime juice, stirring until completely dissolved. Bring back to a rapid boil and when the jelly reaches 104°C/219°F on a sugar thermometer, or when it's been at a vigorous boil for 6–8 minutes, remove from the heat and start set testing (see page 101) for a hard-set jam. If there isn't an evident wrinkle on the plate, return to the heat and keep testing every minute until there is.

Once at the desired set, let it stand for 2–3 minutes, skim off any scum and ladle into hot sterilised jars and seal (see page 15). Turn upside down, allow to set slightly for 25–30 minutes, before turning the right way up so that the chamomile distributes itself evenly throughout the jars. Store unopened in a cool, dark place for up to a year. Once opened, keep in the fridge and eat within 3–4 months.

Quince with a Sage Float

MAKES 6–7 X 230ML/8FL OZ JARS | WINTER | HIGH PECTIN

When making this recipe, remember to keep the leftover
pulp to make a quince paste or cheese (see page 94). You can
easily freeze the pulp if you don't have time to whip up two
quince delights in one day.

2kg/4lb 8oz quince, *peeled,*
  cored and roughly chopped
5–6 strips of pared lemon peel,
  unwaxed
2.5 litres/4½ pints water

700–800g/1lb 9oz–1lb 12oz
  white sugar
60ml lemon juice, *freshly*
  squeezed, strained
6–7 sage leaves, *whole or*
  roughly chopped

Place the prepared quince and lemon peel in a large pot or pan and
completely cover with the water. Simmer over a high heat for 40–50
minutes, then gently crush without over-mashing.

Strain through a large square of muslin tied up by all corners and
suspended over a bowl, or use a jelly bag. Leave for up to 8 hours or
overnight, without being tempted to squeeze the bag.

The next day, sterilise your jars and lids (see page 9) and place several
small saucers in the freezer.

Measure out the quince liquid; for every 200ml/7fl oz of liquid, weigh out 120g/4¼oz of sugar. Pour the juice into a large jam pan with the lemon juice and chopped sage (if using), bring to a rapid boil over the highest heat for about 20 minutes, then stir through the sugar until completely dissolved.

When the jelly reaches 104°C/219°F on a sugar thermometer, or when it's been at a vigorous boil for 16–20 minutes, remove from the heat and start set testing (see page 101) for a hard-set jam. If there isn't an evident wrinkle on the plate, return to the heat and keep testing every minute until there is.

Once at the desired set, let it stand for 2–3 minutes and, if not using chopped sage, set up your hot sterilised jars with a sage leaf in each. Skim off any scum and quickly ladle the jelly into your jars and seal (see page 15). Turn upside down, allow to set slightly for 15–20 minutes, before turning the right way up so that the herbs rise in the jars. Store unopened in a cool, dark place for up to a year. Once opened, keep in the fridge and eat within 3–4 months.

Pretty-in-Pink Zesty Rhubarb Jelly

MAKES 4–5 X 230ML/8FL OZ JARS | WINTER | LOW PECTIN

Use forced rhubarb (the vibrant pink one that's grown by candlelight) if you want the perfect rosy hues of this pretty-in-pink jelly. Rhubarb has next-to-no pectin, so make sure you have the pectin boost of jam sugar, or add rapid-set powdered pectin if you are struggling for a good set.

1.2kg/2lb 11oz forced 'pink' rhubarb, *washed and chopped into 2cm chunks*

1 large Bramley apple, *unwaxed or scrubbed and chopped (with skin, pips and core)*

1.3 litres/2¼ pints water

6 strips of pared lemon peel, *unwaxed*

2–3 limes, *grated zest*

900g–1kg/2lb–2lb 4oz jam sugar

50ml/2fl oz lime juice, *freshly squeezed and strained*

Place the prepared rhubarb and apple in a large pot or pan with the water and lemon peel. Bring to a simmer over a medium heat and after 20 minutes, gently crush the fruit with your wooden spoon, without over-mashing.

Strain through a large square of muslin tied up by all corners and suspended over a bowl, or use a jelly bag. Leave for up to 8 hours or overnight, without being tempted to squeeze the bag.

The next day, sterilise your jars and lids (see page 9) and place several small saucers in the freezer.

Measure out the rhubarb/apple liquid; for every 200ml/7fl oz of liquid, weigh out 160g/5¾oz of sugar. Mix the lime zest through the sugar. Pour the liquid into a jam pan with the lime juice and bring to a rapid boil over the highest heat, then stir through the sugar until completely dissolved.

When the jelly reaches 104°C/219°F on a sugar thermometer, or when it's been at a vigorous boil for 5–6 minutes, remove from the heat and start set testing (see page 101) for a hard set. If there isn't an evident wrinkle on the plate, return to the heat and keep testing every minute until there is.

Once at the desired set, let it stand for 3–4 minutes before skimming off any scum, then quickly ladle into hot sterilised jars and seal (see page 15). Store unopened in a cool, dark place for up to a year. Once opened, keep in the fridge and eat within 3–4 months.

Chapter 4

The Layered Effect

Why choose just one good thing when you can have two, or even three? This chapter gives you the layered effect: for those days when you want the best of both, or a little bit of everything. I call these preserves my 'two-tone' and 'traffic light' jams – named with a little nod to my New Zealand 1980s upbringing.

There's a great photo of my sisters and me when I was five, standing in age and height order, all with matching homemade corduroy overalls (it *was* the early 80s), wearing matching home-knitted red-and-white striped jumpers underneath. Mum in tow, polka dot scarf tying down her bleached-blonde teased hair, all in front of our family's tan and brown, 'two-tone', Ford Cortina.

The Traffic Light was a popular non-alcoholic layered drink, invented by the New Zealand restaurant chain Cobb & Co. Aimed at children, the drink was a big deal for kids in 1980s New Zealand. Red, amber and green, boy did they make you 'go' with the amount of sugar packed into a single pint-sized glass. The Traffic Light was made by first pouring in enough berry cordial or syrup to create a red (stop) layer on the bottom of the glass, filling it with ice, then carefully topping it with an amber layer (orange juice, which is lighter in density so tends to float). Finally, a few drops of green food colouring were added, with a quick stir just on the surface, to create the last green (go) layer.

Much like this layered drink, jam comes in different consistencies and densities, so there is some care and knowledge required to create layers in your jars without them merging into one unrecognisable colour. When just cooked, jam can still be quite loose; it's during the cooling process that the pectin starts to set your preserve. So, there's a juggling act with timings and density at play here in order to get the layers perfectly right.

The following pages offer nine different simple jam recipes, their density rated high (for bottom layers), medium (for middle or top layers) and low (for top layers only). There's also a grid of foolproof layered suggestions, guiding you on timings to start cooking each one. The trick is to check the timings before you start. Start the densest jam to finish first, then gauge when to start the next so that there is about a 4–5-minute break between the two. Carefully ladle the dense layer on the bottom, then a lighter layer 5 minutes after. This gap allows the first jam to set slightly, creating a surface so there's less blending. Gently spoon a couple of teaspoons of the second layer on top first, to gauge the weight before going all the way.

Don't worry about reproducing the traffic light colours every time – this is just semiotics, after all – but if you do want to create a true traffic light effect, try the raspberry, apricot and lime trio.

As they say, practice makes perfect. So, honestly, don't be too stressed if you don't get this right on your first go. I'm one of the most impatient people I know and it took me a few swings at it to get it right. The point is to enjoy the practice of making jam, so relax, take a deep breath and jump right in.

Once you get the hang of this technique and learn the different timings and densities, let yourself discover other combinations to suit your taste and colour palette. These layered-effect jams make great gifts, and it's a fun and novel way of getting two or three jams for the price of one.

A Rainbow of Jams

EACH RECIPE MAKES 3–4 X 230ML/8FL OZ JARS

Splitting into two-tone jars makes 6–8 x 230ml/8fl oz, each jam layer weighing around 120g/4¼oz for a 230ml/8fl oz jar.

Halve the recipe quantity if splitting into three for traffic light jams. Cook in three smaller pans and make sure you have 6–8 sterilised jars prepared and ready to go. Each jam layer should weigh in around 80g/2¾oz for a 230ml/8fl oz jar.

Sterilise enough jars and lids (see page 9) and place several small saucers in the freezer.

The trick is to start with the jam with the longest cooking time, while balancing your timings so that you have 5 minutes for setting before the second or third layer goes on.

Denser jams go on the bottom layers, lighter jams on the top. Make sure you carefully spoon on a surface layer of jam atop another jam, without free pouring – otherwise they can end up blending together. Patience and skill are needed to perfect this technique, so practise, practise, practise.

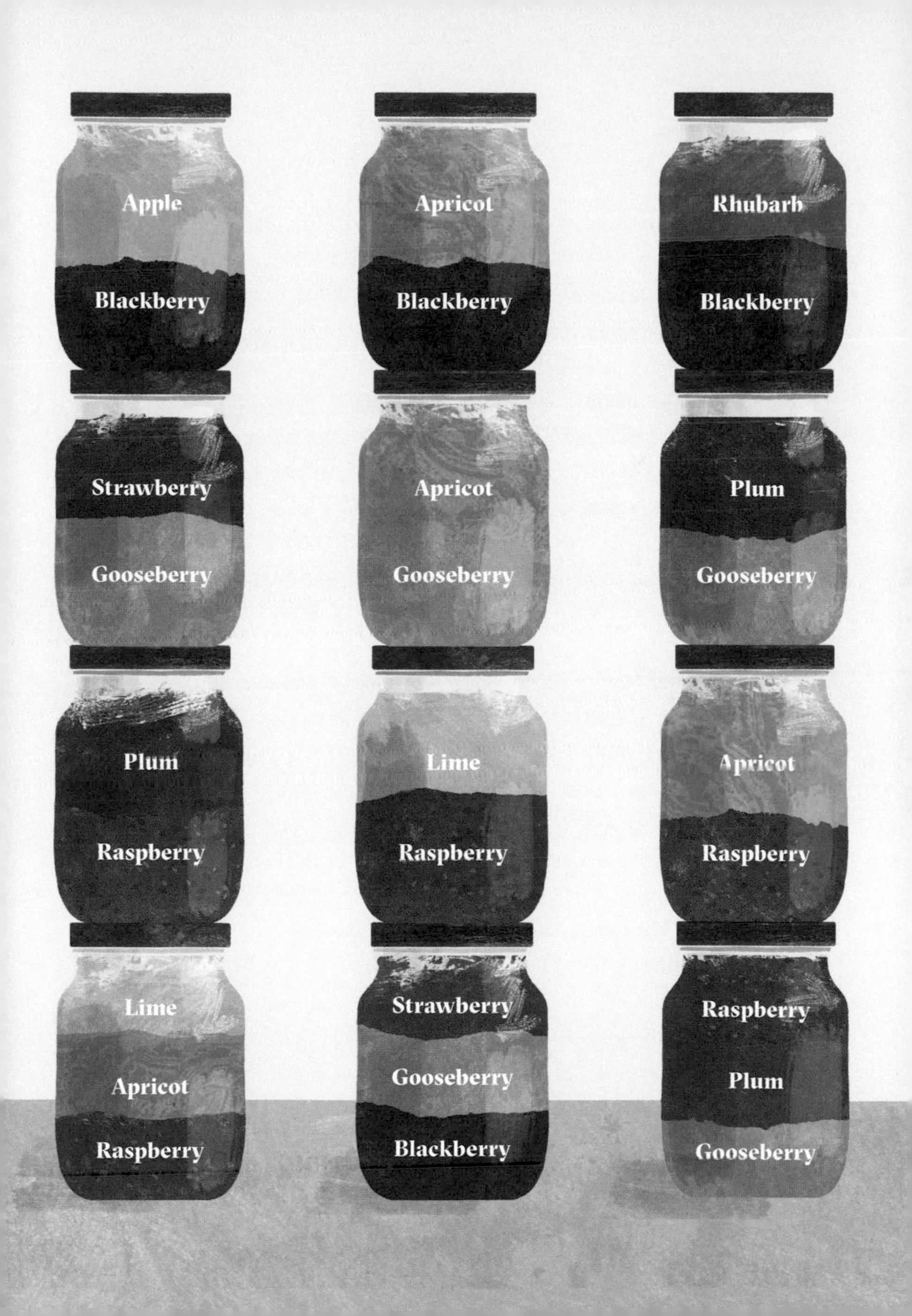
Apple
Blackberry
Apricot
Blackberry
Rhubarb
Blackberry
Strawberry
Gooseberry
Apricot
Gooseberry
Plum
Gooseberry
Plum
Raspberry
Lime
Raspberry
Apricot
Raspberry
Lime
Apricot
Raspberry
Strawberry
Gooseberry
Blackberry
Raspberry
Plum
Gooseberry

Blackberry Jam

600g/1lb 5oz blackberries, *fresh or frozen*
30ml/1fl oz water, *omit if your fruit was frozen*
20ml/¾fl oz lemon juice, *freshly squeezed*
350g/12oz white sugar

Gently rinse your blackberries, defrost if frozen, and place in a jam pan with the water (if using) and lemon juice. Boil for 6–8 minutes, add the sugar, stirring until completely dissolved, then bring back to a vigorous boil and cook for 8–10 minutes. Set test (see page 14) for a hard-set jam, with a clear wrinkle.

Gooseberry Jam

600g/1lb 5oz gooseberries, *top and tailed*
40ml/1¼fl oz water
20ml/¾fl oz lemon juice, *freshly squeezed*
350g/12oz white sugar

Wash the prepared gooseberries and place in a jam pan with the water and lemon juice. Boil for 12–15 minutes until you have a pulp. Add the sugar, stirring until completely dissolved, then bring back to a vigorous boil and cook for 8–10 minutes. Set test (see page 14) for a hard-set jam, with a clear wrinkle.

Raspberry Jam

DENSITY: HIGH | AVERAGE TIMING: 14–18 MINUTES

600g/1lb 5oz raspberries, *gently rinsed*
40ml/1¼fl oz water
20ml/¾fl oz lemon juice, *freshly squeezed*
300g/10½oz white sugar

Place the raspberries in a jam pan with the water and lemon juice.
Gently simmer for 6–8 minutes until you have a pulp. Add the sugar,
stirring until completely dissolved, then bring back to a vigorous boil
and cook for 8–10 minutes. Set test (see page 14) for a hard-set jam,
with a clear wrinkle.

Apple Jam

DENSITY: MEDIUM-HIGH | AVERAGE TIMING: 15–20 MINUTES

700g/1lb 9oz apples, *peeled and cored*
80ml/2¾fl oz water
30ml/1fl oz lemon juice, *freshly squeezed*
350g/12 oz white sugar

Roughly chop the apples into small cubes and place in a jam pan
with the water and lemon juice. Boil for 10–12 minutes until you
have a pulp. Add the sugar, stirring until completely dissolved, then
bring back to a vigorous boil and cook for 5–8 minutes. Set test (see
page 14) for a hard-set jam, with a clear wrinkle.

Rhubarb Jam

DENSITY: MEDIUM | AVERAGE TIMING: 18–22 MINUTES

600g/1lb 5oz pink rhubarb, *forced (if possible)*
50ml/2fl oz water
30ml/1fl oz lemon juice, *freshly squeezed*
350g/12oz jam sugar

Wash and cut the rhubarb into 2cm/¾in pieces. Place in a jam pan
with the water and lemon juice. Boil for 10–12 minutes until you have
a pulp. Add the sugar, stirring until completely dissolved, then bring
back to a vigorous boil and cook for 8–10 minutes. Set test (see page
14) for a soft-set jam, where the jam slowly drops from your finger.

Apricot Jam

DENSITY: MEDIUM | AVERAGE TIMING: 16–20 MINUTES

600g/1lb 5oz apricots, *washed and pitted*
30ml/1fl oz water
20ml/¾fl oz lemon juice, *freshly squeezed*
350g/12oz jam sugar

Cut the apricots into 2cm/¾in cubes and place in a jam pan with the
water and lemon juice. Boil for 8–10 minutes until you have a pulp.
Stir through the sugar, stirring until completely dissolved, then bring
back to a vigorous boil and cook for 8–10 minutes. Set test (see page
14) for a soft-set jam, where the jam slowly drops from your finger.

Plum Jam

DENSITY: MEDIUM | AVERAGE TIMING: 16–20 MINUTES

750g/1lb 10oz plums, *washed and pitted*
30ml/1fl oz water
20ml/¾fl oz lemon juice, *freshly squeezed*
350g/12oz white sugar

Cut the plums into 1–2cm/½–¾in cubes and place in a jam pan with
the water and lemon juice. Boil for 6–8 minutes until you have a
pulp. Stir through the sugar, stirring until completely dissolved, then
bring back to a vigorous boil and cook for 10–12 minutes. Set test
(see page 14) for a hard-set jam, with a clear wrinkle.

Strawberry Jam

DENSITY: LOW | AVERAGE TIMING: 20–25 MINUTES

650g/1lb 7oz strawberries, *rinsed and hulled*
30ml/1fl oz water
20ml/¾fl oz lemon juice, *freshly squeezed*
350g/12oz jam sugar

Wash and quarter the strawberries. Place in a jam pan with the
water and lemon juice. Boil for 8–10 minutes, stirring intermittently,
then stir through the sugar until completely dissolved. Bring back to
a vigorous boil and cook for 12–15 minutes. Set test (see page 14) for
a soft-set jam, where the jam slowly drops from your finger.

Lime Marmalade

DENSITY: LOW | AVERAGE TIMING: 30–32 MINUTES

800g/1lb 12oz juicy limes, *unwaxed or scrubbed*
350ml/12fl oz water
450g/1lb white sugar

Prep the limes by juicing 200g/7oz directly into a jam pan. Carefully slice off the skins of 300g/10½oz limes with a very sharp knife and chop the flesh into 5mm/¼in cubes. Cut the remaining 300g/10½oz limes lengthways down the middle and slice off very fine semicircles (1–2mm in width). Place in a pan with the water and boil for 20 minutes to soften the skins. Stir through the sugar, stirring until completely dissolved, then bring back to a vigorous boil and cook for a further 10 12 minutes. Set test (see page 14) for a hard-set jam, with a clear wrinkle.

Chapter 5

Sundae Fun-day

You've preserved your garden glut, foraged in the wild for ingredients and made the most of the season's bounty. Well done! You have made your food as sustainable as you possibly can by giving it the longevity it deserves.

What's more, you now have a glut of jarred goodies to get through. If you are anything like me, you feel you can only gift so many potted treats to so many people before you've exhausted all your friends. And the pots are still dominating the cupboards. This chapter offers ways to use up your jams, jellies and marmalades in classic jammy 'potted desserts'. These recipes are easy to make and will add a bit of fun to any afternoon tea party, evening feast or children's celebratory birthday bash.

Make sure you are using heatproof jars and to remove any lids, rubber or wire (for your flip-top lids) for the recipes that are baked at temperatures over 180°C/170°C fan/gas 4, so you don't get any exploding glass or burnt rubber.

Strawberry Black Pepper Jammed Eton Mess

MAKES 4 X 300–350ML/10–12FL OZ TALL JARS

For a bit of a twist on this British classic, why not try it with strawberry, balsamic vinegar and black pepper jam? You can use any old strawberry jam you've made or got tucked away in the top shelf of your fridge, but you'll find the black pepper and balsamic vinegar version more subtle and interesting.

250g/9oz strawberries

5 tbsp Strawberry, Balsamic Vinegar and Black Pepper Jam (see page 32)

4 meringue nests, *roughly broken*

200ml/7fl oz double cream, *whipped*

15g/½oz pistachios, *chopped (optional)*

Hull and quarter the strawberries, leaving four whole ones aside for decoration, and place in a bowl. Mix with 4 tablespoons of the jam, cover and macerate for 30 minutes in the fridge.

Assemble the desserts by layering a spoonful of the macerated strawberries into four tall jars to cover the bottom of each. Then add a sprinkling of broken meringue, a spoonful of cream and repeat the layers again in that order. Finish with cream, with a generous drizzle of the leftover jam and a big plump strawberry on top. Sprinkle with the pistachios, if using, and serve with long-handled teaspoons.

Mahonia and Ginger Jelly Trifle

MAKES 4 X 300–350ML/10–12FL OZ WIDE-MOUTHED JARS

Substitute a crystal jelly for a preserve jelly in this not-so-classic version of a trifle. Use any jelly as the base flavour to this recipe; I love this trifle also with the Rosehip and Nasturtium Jelly on page 90.

160g/5¾oz madeira cake or sponge

120ml/4fl oz brandy or sweet vermouth

180–200g/6–7oz cherries, raspberries or strawberries

4–6 tbsp Mahonia and Ginger

Jelly (see page 66) or jelly of your choice

320ml/11fl oz thick custard

240ml/8½fl oz double cream, *whipped*

20g/¾oz flaked almonds, *toasted*

Cut the cake into 1–2cm/½–¾in cubes, place in a bowl and drizzle with the brandy until all the pieces are completely soaked. Divide the soaked pieces of cake between four jars to create the bottom layer of trifle.

Keeping four whole cherries/berries aside, halve the remainder and top the soaked cake with a layer in each jar. Spoon 1–1½ tablespoons of jelly on top, using the back of the spoon to spread it around. Spoon on a thick layer of custard and top off with the whipped cream, then place in the fridge to set for 30 minutes. Serve with a sprinkling of toasted almond flakes and a single cherry or berry on top.

Carrot and Orange Marmalade Bread and Butter Pudding

MAKES 4 X 250–300ML/9–10FL OZ TALL JARS

There's nothing more comforting than comfort food, and bread and butter pudding really hits the spot. Although you can use any marmalade as a substitute in this recipe, do make sure you try it with the spiced carrot version; it could be a game-changer.

10–12 thin slices of brioche or white bread
20–30g/¾ –1oz unsalted butter, *softened*
3–4 tbsp Spiced Carrot Marmalade (see page 54)

10–15g/¼–½ oz raisins (optional)
3 large free-range eggs
220ml/8fl oz double cream
100ml/3½fl oz milk

Preheat the oven to 200°C/190°C fan/gas 6.

Prepare the bread by cutting off any hard crusts, buttering one side and cutting into triangles. Flip the triangles over and spread the marmalade on the other side (this can get messy). Stack the triangles upright in the jars, with the butter facing the back and the triangle points sticking up, sprinkling in raisins as you go (if using).

Whisk the eggs, then whisk in 160ml/5½fl oz of the cream and all of the milk. Pour this mixture over the bread triangles, evenly distributed between the jars, making sure all the bread is soaked. Stand for 5 minutes while it all absorbs.

Bake on a baking sheet in the middle of the oven (remove lids with any rubber seals) for 16–20 minutes until golden brown. Rest for 5 minutes and serve with a drizzle of runny cream over the top, or in a jug on the side.

Blackberry and Rosemary Apple Crumble

MAKES 4 X 300–350ML/10–12FL OZ WIDE-MOUTHED JARS

Crumble is another British classic, and I always add jam to the base of mine. This recipe uses the quintessential combo of blackberry and apple, but try mixing it up. If using apricots in your crumble, try apricot jam, or go wild and make a rhubarb crumble with strawberry jam or a gooseberry crumble with damson jam.

---

2 small apples, *cored, peeled and diced into 1–2cm/½–¾in cubes*

6 tbsp Blackberry and Rosemary Jam (see page 38)

2 tbsp lemon juice, *freshly squeezed*

¼ tsp ground cinnamon

120g/4¼ oz fresh blackberries

80g/2¾oz plain flour

A pinch of sea salt

50g/1¾oz unsalted butter, *chilled, plus extra for greasing*

30g/1oz golden granulated sugar

30g/1oz rolled oats

30g/1oz hazelnuts, *roughly chopped*

4 small sprigs of rosemary

4 scoops vanilla ice cream, *or jug of runny cream*

Put the apples into a bowl and stir through the jam, lemon juice and cinnamon. Add the blackberries, gently coating them in the jam mixture. Cover and leave to macerate for 25–35 minutes.

Mix the flour and the salt in a bowl and rub in the butter with your fingertips until it resembles chunky breadcrumbs, leaving some bigger lumps. Stir through the sugar, oats and hazelnuts. Cover and put into the fridge for 20–30 minutes.

Preheat the oven to 180°C/170°C fan/gas 4. Grease your jars with a little butter.

Assemble the crumbles by dividing the apple and blackberry mixture equally between your jars. Bake on a baking sheet in the middle of the oven for 12 minutes. Remove the tray and generously sprinkle your crumble mix on top of each jar, topping each with a sprig of rosemary, and bake for a further 15-18 minutes or until golden brown. Rest for 5 minutes and serve with a scoop of ice cream or runny double cream.

Apple and Cinnamon Shortcrust Pie Pots

MAKES 4 X 300–350ML/10–12FL OZ WIDE-MOUTHED JARS

*Try making apple pie in a jar with these individual pies so you can
serve just for one – no sharing required. Buy shortcrust pastry for
ease, or have a go at making it yourself for a more homemade feel to
your dessert and to impress your friends.*

160g/5¾oz plain flour, *extra for
dusting*

A pinch of sea salt

80g/2¾oz unsalted butter,
chilled, plus extra for greasing

30g/1oz golden or white caster
sugar

1–2 tbsp milk, *plus extra for
brushing*

4 small apples, *peeled, cored
and diced into 1–2cm/½–¾in
cubes*

12 tbsp Apple and Cinnamon
Jelly (see page 46)

10g/¼oz golden granulated
sugar

4 scoops vanilla ice cream

Mix the flour and salt in a large bowl and rub in the butter with
your fingertips until it resembles fine breadcrumbs. Stir in the sugar
and milk, using your hands to form a ball of dough. Flatten into a
disc, place in an airtight container and place in the fridge for at least
30 minutes.

Dust your work surface with flour and roll the pastry out until it
is 1cm/½in thick. Cut out 4 circles the same size as the inside rim

of your jars. Use the leftover pastry to create leaves or apples to decorate your pie tops. Chill in the fridge for 30 minutes.

Grease your jars with a little butter. Place the prepared apples in a saucepan with the jelly and 2 tablespoons of water and simmer over a medium heat for 5-6 minutes, stirring until softened.

Assemble the pie pots by dividing the cooked apple between your jars, then leave to cool. Place a chilled pastry disc and any decorative pastry pieces on top of each, then make a slit with a sharp knife in the tops and chill again for 30 minutes.

Preheat the oven to 180°C/170°C fan/gas 4. Brush the pie tops with milk and bake in the middle of the oven for 20-25 minutes until golden on top. Sprinkle with the granulated sugar and rest for 10 minutes before serving with vanilla ice cream on top.

Plum and Hazelnut Swirl Cheesecake

MAKES 4 X 250–300ML/9–10FL OZ WIDE-MOUTHED JARS

Cheesecake in a pot. Perfection in a jar. Easy, quick-to-make, effortless no-bake desserts in 1½ hours. Make the night before so you can whip out, dress and impress.

140g/5oz digestive biscuits
30g/1oz hazelnuts, *toasted, finely chopped*
A pinch of sea salt
70g/2½oz unsalted butter, *melted*

500g/1lb 2oz full-fat cream cheese
50g/1¾oz icing sugar
110ml double cream, *whipped to soft peaks*
5 tbsp Red Plum and Hazelnut Jam (see page 26)

Crush the digestives in a food processor, or in a bag with a rolling pin, to a fine crumb. Stir through the hazelnuts and salt and pour over the melted butter, mixing until the crumbs are completely covered. Evenly press the crumb gently into the base of four jars and chill in the fridge for at least 30 minutes.

In a large bowl, beat the cream cheese and icing sugar together with an electric whisk until smooth and the mixture starts to thicken – at least 2–3 minutes. Fold through the whipped cream and, once the texture holds its shape and doesn't drip off the spoon, gently fold in 4 tablespoons of the plum jam in two batches to create a swirl effect.

Carefully spoon the mix into your jars, pushing it down to eliminate any air bubbles, and smooth off the tops with a spatula. Clean around the glass rims with a damp cloth and refrigerate overnight.

Take the cheesecakes out of the fridge 5–10 minutes before serving. Make a quick syrup by mixing the remaining jam with 2–3 tablespoons of water. Drizzle over the tops of the cheesecakes just before serving.

Cherry and Cacao Nib Pot Brownies

MAKES 4 X 250–300ML/9–10FL OZ WIDE-MOUTHED JARS

Most people can't go past a brownie, so surprise them with a jam-swirled pot brownie (the child-friendly type).

130g/4½oz unsalted butter, *plus extra for greasing*

130g/4½oz dark chocolate, 70% *(or more) cocoa solids*

40g/1½oz cocoa powder

3 large free-range eggs

160g/5¾ oz golden or white granulated sugar

90g/3¼oz plain flour

A pinch of sea salt

6–8 tsp Cherry and Cacao Nib Jam (see page 30)

Crème fraîche or vanilla ice cream, *to serve*

Preheat the oven to 180°C/170°C fan/gas 4. Grease your jars with a little butter. Chop the butter and chocolate and melt in the microwave or over a bain-marie. Whisk through the cocoa powder and set aside to cool.

In a large bowl, whisk the eggs, slowly adding the sugar, until thickened and pale. Fold through the chocolate mixture until smooth. Sift in the flour and salt and then fold until combined. Spoon the batter halfway up your prepared jars, then add 2 heaped teaspoons of jam to each, swirling with the handle of a teaspoon. Bake in the middle of the oven for 22–24 minutes so that the top has a crust but still with a gentle wobble. Once ready, cool for 10 minutes and serve with crème fraîche or a scoop of ice cream.

Grapefruit Aperol Spritz Baked Rice Pudding

MAKES 4 X 300–350ML/10–12FL OZ WIDE-MOUTHED JARS

Baked rice pudding is another classic dessert. It's easy to halve the quantities of this recipe to make just two portions.

1–2 tsp unsalted butter
240ml/8½fl oz double cream
600ml/1 pint milk
50g/1¾oz golden or white sugar

240g/8½oz pudding rice
40g/1½oz raisins
4–6 tsp Ruby Grapefruit Aperol Spritz Marmalade (see page 52)

In a large saucepan, mix together the cream, milk and sugar with the rice. Gently bring to a simmer on a medium-low heat, stirring intermittently, for about 30 minutes, then stir through the raisins.

Preheat the oven to 160°C/150°C fan/gas 3. Grease your jars with the butter and spoon the creamed rice mixture equally between four jars. Gently swirl through a heaped teaspoon of marmalade into each. Bake on a baking sheet in the middle of the oven for 35–40 minutes.

Carefully remove halfway through baking and give a gentle stir, mixing in any skin that may have formed on top. When the rice is cooked and tender with a slight bite (different ovens will vary in timings) it is ready. Rest for 5 minutes and then serve.

Scones with Cream and Rhubarb and Rose Jam

MAKES 4 X 250–300ML/9–10FL OZ WIDE-MOUTHED JARS

High tea, anyone? How do you eat your scone? For those of us who can't decide whether it should be cream or jam first, then just go for the layered effect to appease all tastes and types.
Feel free to buy the scones to save on time.

120g/4¼oz self-raising flour, *plus extra for dusting*
A small pinch of sea salt
2 tsp caster sugar
25g/1oz unsalted butter, *chilled and cubed*

100–120ml/3 ½–4fl oz milk, *room temperature*
200ml/7fl oz double cream, *lightly whipped*
8 tbsp Rhubarb and Rose Jam (see page 42) or jam of your choice

---

Preheat the oven to 220°C/200°C fan/gas 7. Line a baking sheet with baking paper and lightly dust with flour.

Mix the flour, salt and sugar in a large bowl and rub in the butter with your fingertips until it resembles fine breadcrumbs. Mix in a bit of the milk at a time with a butter knife until the mixture just comes together – it should not be too tacky but not too dry either.

Turn the dough out onto a lightly dusted surface and shape into a round, then flatten so that it's about 2cm thick. Choose a round

cutter 1cm/½in smaller than the diameter of your jars and gently twist and press into the dough to make 4 scones.

Place them close together on the prepared baking sheet and bake for 10–12 minutes until golden. Once ready, leave to cool before slicing in half. Put the bottom slices first into your jars, then cream or jam; stack the other half on top, followed by jam or cream. Dealer's choice.

Raspberry and Amaretto Arctic Stacks

MAKES 4 X 300–350ML/10–12FL OZ TALL JARS

Depending on your baking skills, you can use the sponge recipe below and make it from scratch or you may have a go-to sponge recipe already. Alternatively, simply use a pre-made sponge or madeira cake to attempt this take on the classic Arctic roll.

Unsalted butter, *for greasing*
2 large, free-range eggs
90g/3¼oz golden or white
  caster sugar
90g/3¼oz plain flour
½ tsp baking powder

¼ tsp vanilla extract
4 scoops vanilla ice cream
8–10 tbsp Raspberry and
  Amaretto Jam (see page 34)
  or jam of your choice

Preheat the oven to 200°C/190°C fan/gas 6. Grease and line a 28 x 18cm/11 x 7in baking tin with baking paper.

In a large bowl, whisk the eggs with an electric whisk and slowly add the sugar until dissolved, thickened and pale. Mix the flour with the baking powder and gently fold through the egg and sugar mixture, a spoonful at a time, then stir in the vanilla extract until just combined.

Pour into the prepared tin and bake in the middle of the oven for 10–12 minutes or until lightly golden and springy to the touch. Remove and allow to cool for 20 minutes. Remove the ice cream from the freezer to soften for 15 minutes.

Once the sponge has cooled, cut out 12 circles with a cookie cutter, the same diameter as your jars. Spread a thick layer of jam over the tops of 8 circles and on both sides of the remaining 4 circles. Carefully place a sponge circle jam-side up in each jar, add a large scoop of ice cream on top, then a double-sided jammed sponge, another scoop of ice cream and end with the last sponge with the jam side facing down.

Seal, with the lids pressing the puddings into the jars to gently compact them, and place in the freezer for 30 minutes. Remove from the freezer 6–10 minutes before serving.

Greengage and Lemon Thyme Jam Possets

MAKES 4 X 200ML/7FL OZ TALL JARS

There's something about the tartness of lemon posset; it can hit you in the face and make you scrunch up all your features. That's why I like to add a little jammy sweetness to the bottom of mine: to soften the blow, so to speak.

---

6 tbsp Greengage and Lemon Thyme Jam (see page 24) or any jam of your choice
500ml/18fl oz double cream
90g/3¼oz golden or white caster sugar

2 lemons, grated zest
70ml/2½fl oz lemon juice
30g/1oz cornflakes, *gently crushed*
Lemon thyme leaves, *to garnish*

Put a heaped tablespoon of jam in each jar.

In a medium saucepan, bring the cream to a gentle simmer and once you start to see steam and small bubbles, stir through the sugar until dissolved. Simmer over a medium heat for 1 minute, take off the heat, stir through the lemon zest and juice and rest for 1–2 minutes.

Pour the warm liquid posset into a jug before dividing slowly and evenly between your jars. Cool before chilling in the fridge for at least 4 hours. Serve straight from the fridge with crushed cornflakes on top for texture and a sprinkle of lemon thyme leaves to garnish

Lemon Syllabub with Peach and Basil Jam

MAKES 4 X 200–230ML/7–8FL OZ TALL JARS

With a few simple ingredients, you can whip up a classy dessert like a syllabub. I find a bit of sweetness from the jam and the crunch of the amaretti biscuits are welcome additions to this classic tart dessert.

90ml /3fl oz white wine
20ml/¾fl oz brandy
1 lemon, *zested*
30ml/1fl oz lemon juice
50g/1¾oz golden or white
   caster sugar

260ml/9½fl oz double cream
80–100g/2¾–3½oz amaretti
   biscuits, *gently crushed*
8 heaped tsp Peach and Basil
   Jam (see page 22)
4 small sprigs of mint

Place the wine, brandy, lemon zest and juice with the sugar in a bowl and stir until the sugar has completely dissolved. Cover and macerate for 1–2 hours, then strain.

In a large bowl, whisk the cream with the strained liquid and beat for at least 6 minutes until it starts to hold its shape. In a smaller bowl, mix the broken amaretti biscuits with the jam, reserving some crumbs to decorate the tops. Divide the jammy crumbs between your four jars, top evenly with the syllabub and refrigerate for at least 2 hours. Serve with a sprinkling of the reserved amaretti crumbs and a sprig of mint.

Index